Cambridge Elements

Elements in New Religious Movements
edited by
James R. Lewis
Wuhan University
Rebecca Moore
San Diego State University

PEOPLES TEMPLE AND JONESTOWN IN THE TWENTY-FIRST CENTURY

Rebecca Moore
San Diego State University

CAMBRIDGE
UNIVERSITY PRESS

CAMBRIDGE
UNIVERSITY PRESS

University Printing House, Cambridge CB2 8BS, United Kingdom

One Liberty Plaza, 20th Floor, New York, NY 10006, USA

477 Williamstown Road, Port Melbourne, VIC 3207, Australia

314–321, 3rd Floor, Plot 3, Splendor Forum, Jasola District Centre, New Delhi – 110025, India

103 Penang Road, #05–06/07, Visioncrest Commercial, Singapore 238467

Cambridge University Press is part of the University of Cambridge.

It furthers the University's mission by disseminating knowledge in the pursuit of education, learning, and research at the highest international levels of excellence.

www.cambridge.org
Information on this title: www.cambridge.org/9781009015899
DOI: 10.1017/9781009032025

© Rebecca Moore 2022

First published 2022

A catalogue record for this publication is available from the British Library.

ISBN 978-1-009-01589-9 Paperback
ISSN 2635-232X (online)
ISSN 2635-2311 (print)

Peoples Temple and Jonestown in the Twenty-First Century

Elements in New Religious Movements

DOI: 10.1017/9781009032025
First published online: August 2022

Rebecca Moore
San Diego State University
Author for correspondence: Rebecca Moore, remoore@sdsu.edu

Abstract: The new religious movement of Peoples Temple, begun in the 1950s, came to a dramatic end with the mass murders and suicides that occurred in Jonestown, Guyana, in 1978. This analysis presents the historical context for understanding the Temple by focusing on the ways that migrations from Indiana to California and finally to the Cooperative Republic of Guyana shaped the life and thought of Temple members. It closely examines the religious beliefs, political philosophies, and economic commitments held by the group, and it shifts the traditional focus on the leader and founder, Jim Jones, to the individuals who made up the heart and soul of the movement. It also investigates the paradoxical role that race and racism played throughout the life of the Temple. The Element concludes by considering the ways in which Peoples Temple and the tragedy at Jonestown have entered the popular imagination and captured international attention.

Keywords: new religious movements, Peoples Temple, Jonestown, religion and violence, brainwashing, cults, anticult movement

ISBNs: 9781009015899 (PB), 9781009032025 (OC)
ISSNs: 2635-232X (online), 2635-2311 (print)

Contents

Introduction

More than forty years ago, people around the world were shocked to learn of the mass murders and suicides of more than nine hundred Americans who belonged to an obscure religious group. A thousand members of Peoples Temple, based in California, had emigrated to the South American country of Guyana and settled in the remote community of Jonestown, named after their leader, Jim Jones. Residents of Jonestown believed that a group of conspirators wanted to destroy their communal village, and they saw the proof of that in the unwelcome visit of Congressman Leo J. Ryan of California. As the congressman and his party prepared to leave following the visit, gunmen acting on Jones's command attacked them at a jungle airstrip six miles from Jonestown. They killed Ryan, three journalists, and one defecting Temple member. Back in Jonestown, a well-rehearsed plan to take poison went into operation as adults murdered their children before – willingly or unwillingly – ingesting poison themselves. More than one hundred and twenty-five miles away in the capital city of Guyana, another Temple member killed her three children and herself under orders coming via shortwave radio from Jonestown. At the end of November 18, 1978, nine hundred and fourteen Temple members had perished along with Congressman Ryan and three others.

Despite its historical distance, this singular event reverberates in countless ways in the present. More than eighty nonfiction books on the topic have been published in English with dozens more in other languages. Countless articles, both scholarly and popular, have analyzed the catastrophe. Documentaries, fiction films, dramas, novels, podcasts, and blogs continue to interpret the events in a variety of factual and counterfactual ways. If anything, the story of Peoples Temple and the deaths in Jonestown is overdetermined.

It is therefore fair to ask if another work about Jonestown is necessary. This account takes up the challenge of presenting a brief yet comprehensive analysis of Peoples Temple and its attempt to create a new society in Jonestown. Public appetite for cult stories has exploded in the era of NXIVM and QAnon. Indeed, more than one moral panic has recently arisen involving fear of cults (e.g., Reichert & Richardson 2012; Krinsky 2016; Cusack 2020). Anxiety over extreme religious commitment – frequently characterized as "belonging to a cult" – often evokes the specter of violence, especially mass suicide. Thus a fresh assessment of Peoples Temple and Jonestown is needed to eradicate misconceptions and show how atypical the group was and remains.

Another reason for examining Peoples Temple anew is that documents released under the Freedom of Information Act (FOIA) continue to be published, offering insights into the inner workings of the group. The vast majority of items were not made available to the public before the turn of the twenty-first century. It was difficult to get accurate information in the middle of a mass tragedy, so factual errors plagued initial news reports. Many have been corrected thanks to reliable documents released under FOIA. Unfortunately, much of the misinformation published more than four decades ago is still being reproduced, amplified by internet memes, websites, and bloggers. This problem is exacerbated by recent oral histories in which individuals recount the experiences of forty years earlier and introduce factual errors. The problem of misremembering details, or not having information in the first place, remains a potential drawback when relying on oral accounts. People change their stories over time. FOIA documents show the messy process of reacting to a major disaster, with moment-by-moment updates and corrections. Errors remain, but they can frequently be spotted with the help of 20/20 hindsight.

Because the present Element relies on the most current scholarship regarding Peoples Temple in particular, and new religious movements in general, it has advantages lacking in the earliest eyewitness statements. Primary-source written documents such as cables, government reports, letters, audiotapes, and other items – even some news stories – frequently offer more accurate insights than recollections articulated four decades later. One of the most interesting sources acquired through FOIA is a collection of journals written by Temple member Edith Roller and discovered in Jonestown after the tragedy. Written between 1975 and 1978, these revealing diaries described experiences both mundane and extraordinary. Most importantly, they were not colored by any ex post facto analyses of the deaths in Jonestown. A true believer, Roller lived her life committed to social change. She provided prosaic descriptions of food she ate, classes she taught, chores she performed, and books she read. She even described at least one suicide rehearsal before she perished on November 18.

Former Temple members whose memoirs of life in the Temple have come out since the year 2000 are also challenging long-accepted narratives. Like Edith Roller, they offer rarely seen vistas on life among the rank and file (e.g., Kohl 2010), in contrast to the viewpoints of apostate leaders and critics. In addition, many survivors – both defectors who left before the end and loyalists who averted death by not being present in Jonestown on the final day – have published personal reflections in the Alternative Considerations of Jonestown and Peoples Temple (Alternative Considerations), a digital archive hosted by San Diego State University. These articles and remembrances present a look inside the Temple that goes beyond headlines by presenting insights into day-to-day life within the group. All of these memoirs and reflections enlarge our understanding of what Peoples Temple was and how members functioned within it.

Historically, the voices of Black members of Peoples Temple were erased, drowned out by more vocal and visible spokespersons (Moore 2018b). As journalist Jamilah King observed in 2018, "Jonestown is largely seen as a white catastrophe" (King 2018). This is especially problematic given the fact that almost three-quarters of those who died in Jonestown were Black and that 90 percent of Temple members in the United States were African American. But contemporary Black writers, poets, and artists are significantly extending the field of vision for understanding the importance of the Temple in US history and religious consciousness (e.g., Wagner-Wilson 2008; Gillespie 2011; Hutchinson 2015; E. Smith 2021; scott 2022). The republication of some of the earliest African American evaluations, along with new analyses, also reinscribed Black voices into the understanding of Jonestown (Moore, Pinn & Sawyer 2004; Kwayana 2016).

The first descriptions of Peoples Temple and Jonestown in the aftermath largely came from White defectors, or ex-members, who had little sympathy for and even less experience with the purposes and goals of Peoples Temple. Many were part of a group called Concerned Relatives who sought to remove family members from the Temple. The Concerned Relatives were influenced by a national anticult movement dedicated to exposing the dangers and abuses that existed in some new religions. Their voices dominated media coverage of the deaths in Jonestown and prompted reporters to frame the story of Peoples Temple as one of fraud and fakery rather than one of failed ideals and thwarted hopes. Justifiable outrage over the murder of almost four hundred young adults, teenagers, children and infants made it virtually impossible to countenance any other perspective. At the same time, the outrage paradoxically hindered sorely needed criminal investigations and scholarly analyses.

The twenty-first century has also seen greater appreciation for narratives from Guyana, the South American country in which the calamity occurred. Most Guyanese had never heard of Jonestown before the nation was rocked with news of the deaths of more than nine hundred Americans on their soil. While some contemporary opinion pieces criticized the Guyana government, few in the United States or in the international community knew of these critiques. A year after the deaths, Guyana nationalist Walter Rodney (1942–80) gave a talk at Stanford University in which he blamed the government of Guyana for the deaths in Jonestown (Rodney 1979). His talk, coupled with evaluations by additional government critics, was collected and republished by another Guyana nationalist, Eusi Kwayana (Kwayana 2016). Moreover, literary works by Guyanese authors have made Guyana, rather than the United States, the center of the Jonestown story. They tend to locate the deaths in Jonestown within a postcolonial context that has generally been ignored.

Recent interviews with Guyanese individuals who were present at the Port Kaituma airstrip or in Jonestown shortly before or after the deaths have cleared up several mysteries. For example, the first Guyana official to reach the death scene provided an initial body count of four hundred people. He based his evaluation on the fact that he was told that four hundred passports were found, rather than on an actual count (M. Johnson 2019). This preliminary guesstimate created the misapprehension that hundreds of people fled into the jungle, a mistake corrected only in the days that followed as more bodies were uncovered during the process of recovering the remains.

For more than forty years, scholars have investigated the Temple and Jonestown from myriad angles (Levi 1982b; Weightman 1984; Maaga 1998; Chidester 2003; Hall 2004; Moore 2018a). General assessments of violence occurring in new religions have also contributed to understanding the events in Jonestown (Hall 1995; Hall with Schuyler & Trinh 2000; Wessinger 2000; Moore 2011 and 2018d). A range of articles has investigated the Temple movement from the perspectives of psychology (e.g., Lasaga 1980; A. Smith 1982; Ulman & Abse 1983; Nesci 1999 and 2018), sociology (e.g., P. Johnson 1979; Hall 1988; Feltmate 2016 and 2018), and religious studies (e.g., Levi 1982a; Chidester 1988; Klippenstein 2015 and 2018; Folk 2018). All of these studies, and many more, go far beyond the immediate journalistic reports (e.g., Kilduff & Javers 1978; Krause 1978) and popular interpretations (e.g., Kerns with Wead 1979; Nugent 1979) that emerged in the weeks and months after November 1978.

Two high-quality mass-market books serve as bookends distinguished by care, attention, and in-depth research, in contrast to dozens of sensationalistic accounts. Reporter Tim Reiterman of the *San Francisco Examiner* was wounded at the Port Kaituma airstrip on November 18 as he covered Congressman Leo Ryan's visit. While the coauthored volume *Raven* starts from the premise that Jim Jones was troubled "from the very beginning" (Reiterman with Jacobs 1982: 5), it still provides a wealth of detail lacking in any prior books. Thirty-five years later, Jeff Guinn retraced Reiterman and Jacobs's footsteps in *The Road to Jonestown* (Guinn 2017). But Guinn, also a journalist, took a different approach and came up with new details that clarified the role of Jim Jones within the larger Peoples Temple movement. His focus on members, rather than just the leader, broadened popular understanding of both.

Finally, the Alternative Considerations digital archive, established in 1998, has made thousands of documents, articles, personal reflections, video reports, audiotapes and transcripts, genealogical trees, and other items publicly available for more than two decades. Hosted by Special Collections at the San Diego State University Library, it has become an essential stop for researchers, family

Figure 1 Children and young adults in Peoples Temple Redwood Valley branch, 1975. Photo by Claire Janaro. Courtesy of the Jonestown Institute

members, and others looking into the life and death of Peoples Temple. Digitization has internationalized the scope of Jonestown research and has centralized much of the information by publishing it online in a single clearing-house. (Full disclosure: The author and the author's husband, Fielding McGehee III, manage this website under the name the Jonestown Institute. Their interest in Peoples Temple stems in part from the deaths of the author's sisters Carolyn Layton and Annie Moore and Carolyn's son Kimo Prokes in Jonestown.) The California Historical Society also maintains an extensive archive of Temple documents, including thousands of photographs taken during the group's existence.

In light of these developments, a reappraisal of Peoples Temple and Jonestown is both timely and necessary. Section 1 begins with a brief history of Peoples Temple and its demise in Jonestown. It discusses the origins of the Temple in Indianapolis, Indiana, under the leadership of Jim Jones and his wife, Marceline Baldwin Jones, noting the significance of race and class. The section presents the reasons for the migration of about one hundred and forty people from Indiana to rural northern California in the mid-1960s, along with its expansion to the urban centers of San Francisco and Los Angeles. It traces the relocation of a significant portion of the group from the United States to the Cooperative Republic of Guyana, beginning in 1974 and culminating with the emigration of a thousand people in 1977 and 1978. The influence of the Concerned Relatives and the role played by US government agencies are examined before turning to the final weeks and days of the movement.

After providing this background, the Element scrutinizes the group through three different analytical lenses: religious, political, and economic. What was the Temple exactly? A religious group? A political organization? A social movement? An intentional community? A dangerous cult? To greater or lesser degrees, the answer to all of these questions is yes, but it is a yes that affirms the complex nature of Peoples Temple and its members. It was indeed a religious group with political and social ambitions that encouraged its members to lead exemplary lives of commitment. In that respect, as a high-demand group living an encapsulated existence in the jungles of a foreign country under the guidance of a charismatic leader, it looks like a stereotypical cult. But that brief description fails to do justice to the yearnings of the majority of the group's members. A closer look at particular dimensions is needed.

Section 2 surveys the varieties of religious experience in Peoples Temple. The complicated psychology and philosophy of the group's leader, Jim Jones – a White man with a strong sense of economic and social grievance – has been the mainstay of many analyses, particularly those appearing in mass media. This emphasis on the leader neglects the enormous influence of Black religion and culture upon the movement. Thus we find elements of the historic Black Church, New Thought, liberal Protestantism, and Humanism at different moments in the religious history of Peoples Temple. Yet all make up what religion scholar Anthony Pinn identifies as various modalities of Black religion (Pinn 2004).

The situation of the times shaped the political outlook of the Temple, especially in the 1970s, the subject of Section 3. While the group presented itself as a church to the world, its more radical political commitments were largely concealed. Members did participate in activities acceptable under the Christian social gospel, such as demonstrating peacefully for racial equality and writing letters to public officials. With the collapse of the civil rights movement in the sixties and the emergence of Black Power in the seventies, however, activists grew more militant in their demands, with the Temple no less vocal. A belief that true commitment required dying for the Cause arose among many social activists. The Cause may have been human liberation, equality, and dignity for Black activists in the United States or, in the case of Peoples Temple members, socialism and their own community. Black Panther leader Huey Newton succinctly articulated this view in the expression "revolutionary suicide" (Newton 1973). Newton meant that if one challenges an unjust system, one must face the likelihood of dying – not unrealistic given the number of assassinations of Black leaders that occurred throughout the 1950s, 1960s, and 1970s. With the move to Guyana, Temple members espoused an explicitly socialist and communist agenda in the hope that they would immigrate to the Soviet Union and avoid the fate of other radicals.

Section 4 explores the eminently successful economic organization of Peoples Temple across its twenty-five-year history. Beginning with profitable care homes run by Marceline Jones in Indianapolis, continuing with group homes in Redwood Valley, California, foster parenting payments, and life care income from senior citizens in San Francisco, Peoples Temple was able to mobilize not only capital but also labor in efficient ways. Peer pressure encouraged members to donate valuable real estate, jewelry, assets, and property to the group as evidence of their unwavering commitment to the Cause. Working for income-generating projects like running thrift stores, panhandling for contributions, selling the *Peoples Forum* newspaper, and operating a printing press for outside customers were just a few of the ways the Temple made money in the United States. With the move to Guyana, the group became more dependent upon the Social Security income provided by senior citizens since no one in Jonestown had an outside job. Jonestown residents ran a small store along the Kaituma River to raise funds, and members in Georgetown took to the streets to beg for money to support the agricultural mission. They came up with a variety of money-making schemes, while Temple members back in the United States were urged to collect larger offerings at church services. By marshalling unpaid labor to do all of the construction, maintenance, farm work, feeding, and more to maintain the project, the group was very successful, at least for a time. Had Jones and his leaders invested some of the millions of dollars stashed in foreign banks into day-to-day living in Jonestown, life there would have been easier.

The concluding section reflects upon the afterlives of Peoples Temple. Although the institution went into official bankruptcy by the end of 1978, with no successor organization, it nevertheless has had an ongoing life in the public mind. Clearly interest in Peoples Temple remains high, with new books, documentaries, and literary works appearing every year, especially on the anniversary date of the Jonestown deaths. From the production of the drama *Jonestown* by an Iranian playwright, to the display of a nine-by-twelve-foot handcrafted "Jonestown Carpet" by a Canadian performance artist, to the composition of Frank Zappa's symphonic composition "Jonestown," Peoples Temple and its demise seem to resonate deeply with artists working in a wide variety of mediums. Section 5 explains this ongoing fascination with Peoples Temple and Jonestown.

This Element also considers the approaches that scholars have taken to assess the impact of the deaths. Researchers have analyzed the elements leading to the violence in Jonestown and conducted comparative studies of violent outbursts involving other new religions. Jonestown was a boon to anticult activists since it seemed to confirm their belief that all new religions had the potential for mass murder and suicide (Moore 2018c). Yet anticult agitation led directly to the US government's tragic handling of the Branch Davidians at Waco in 1993, according to one scholar (Hall 1995). Pseudo-scholarly theories also continue to circulate on the Internet, despite efforts to debunk them. Thus Jonestown lives on.

One organizing principle that runs throughout this Element is that of migration – from Indiana to California to Guyana. We might even mark an earlier migration with the mass movement of African Americans from the South to the North in the early twentieth century. These different locations mark distinct eras in the ideology, program, and practices of the group. The life of any organization – and of any individual, for that matter – changes according to historical events, geographical location, and surrounding culture. Peoples Temple was no different. That is why it is imperative to clarify which period is under consideration and where. Following the typology developed by sociologist Ernst Troeltsch, religion historian Mary Maaga identified three groups within the Temple movement. There was the Indianapolis sect, the Redwood Valley new religious movement (or cult), and the Black Church of San Francisco and Los Angeles (Maaga 1998: 74–86). While there are advantages to taking this approach, it neglects the identity of Peoples Temple in Guyana, which should be characterized as a utopian communal experiment based in Humanistic thought. Therefore this Element abandons the sect-cult-church typology and adopts instead the three transformative environments in which the Temple operated: Indiana, California, and Guyana.

As differentiated from many depictions of Peoples Temple, this account also investigates the importance of race along with migration in understanding the movement. The Temple started as an intentionally integrated church in a time of formal and informal segregation. It deliberately cultivated Black membership throughout its existence and valorized Blackness – at least rhetorically. In reality a White hierarchy dominated the decision-making process. Nevertheless African Americans ultimately remained the heart of the movement, not only numerically but also in terms of development, accomplishment, and ideology.

Finally, the Element attempts to remove Jim Jones from the center of the Peoples Temple story. Jones has epitomized the evil cult leader, not only in popular culture but also in the scholarly literature that emphasizes the role of the charismatic leader in new religions. While it is true that the movement began and ended with him and his vision, that is only a partial truth. His wife, Marceline Jones, played an important role throughout the Temple's history, as did the members who brought their own experiences, hopes, and aspirations to the group. Focusing on Jones ignores the dynamics between leader and disciples and neglects the significance of followers in shaping the Temple movement.

The deaths in Jonestown will always remain a warning against the dangers of ignoring individual conscience over the demands of group ideology and of disregarding ethical norms in pursuit of transcendent goals. But the lives in Peoples Temple tell another story, one to which this Element turns.

1 The Life and Death of Peoples Temple

Because of the tragic events at Jonestown, the commune's name has come to represent everything there is to know about Peoples Temple. The reality, however, is that the social, geographical, and historical context of each location in which the Temple existed shaped its character in fundamental ways. "Evolving residential patterns (individual, enclave, communal) marked the institutional organization of Peoples Temple over its twenty-five year history" (Moore 2022b). Political issues, such as civil rights and national liberation in the United States and abroad, guided the Temple's social activism. Indiana in the 1950s differed greatly from California in the 1960s and 1970s. Guyana – a foreign country, a distinct culture, and a new setting – presented the most challenges. The demographics of Peoples Temple evolved along the way, shifting from a majority-White institution to majority Black. This section examines the ways in which the movement changed in its various locations until its final day.

Indiana

The story of Peoples Temple began in the American Midwest with two remarkable individuals. James Warren Jones (1931–78) and Marceline Mae Baldwin

Jones (1927–78) were born and raised in Indiana. The two differed in almost every respect: social class, family upbringing, religious commitment. But they did share a concern for the underdog. They met at Reid Memorial Hospital in Richmond, Indiana, where Marceline was training to be a nurse and Jim, a high school student, worked at night as a hospital orderly. They married in 1949 in a double ceremony with Marceline's sister Eloise, who wedded Dale Klingman.

Sources are few for Marceline despite the important role she played in the development of the Temple (see, however, Reiterman with Jacobs 1982; S. Jones 2005; Guinn 2017; Shearer 2020). A common observation, however, is that she was kind, caring, and self-sacrificing. These qualities led her into the field of nursing. She was also extremely competent, a shrewd administrator who became both an excellent breadwinner and an astute financial manager in the Temple's early days. Jones claimed to have "built and established" a nursing home with his own money in Indianapolis (J. Jones 1977), but it was Marceline and another White woman, Esther Mueller, who turned the Jones's home into a care facility (Guinn 2017). Marceline maintained steady administrative positions in California that supported the family. Once the group moved to Guyana, she served as an emissary between the outposts there and in the United States, a leading presence at the Jonestown health clinic, and "the compassionate heart of Peoples Temple" (Cartmell 2010). Marceline Jones was a complex figure, however, participating in faked healings (Thielmann with Merrill 1979; Harpe 2010), knowingly turning a blind eye to her husband's sexual infidelities, and concealing the rape of a fourteen-year-old girl (e.g., Stoen 1972; FBI Audiotape Q775 1973).

In contrast to the dearth of information on Marceline, popular analyses of Jim abound, frequently portraying him in broad strokes as an evil charlatan whose apparent piety masked a vindictive and sadistic brutishness (e.g., Maguire & Dunn 1978; Mills 1979; Scheeres 2011). Accounts of cruelty to animals when he was a boy indicate a mean streak (Reiterman with Jacobs 1982; Guinn 2017), while audiotapes made in Jonestown vividly reveal Jim Jones at his most vicious and abusive.

These sources are of course at odds with the personal reflections of Jim Jones and his family. His mother, Lynetta Putnam Jones (1902/4–78), wrote brief stories about her own life in Lynn, Indiana, along with short, affectionate sketches of her son's early life (L. Jones n.d.). Many stories that we might call "Temple lore" originated with Jim, Marceline, and Lynetta, such as his avowal to have walked out of a barber shop that discriminated against a Black man (M. Jones & L. Jones 1975). But other tales that achieved legendary status were true, such as the time he was assigned to a Black hospital ward as a patient and

Figure 2 James Warren Jones and Marceline Mae Baldwin Jones, Redwood Valley, date unknown. Courtesy of the Special Collections and University Archives, San Diego State University Library

refused to be moved to the White ward. The incident prompted the hospital to desegregate its wards (Reiterman with Jacobs 1982: 75–6).

What is clear from numerous accounts is that Jim Jones identified strongly with the poor and disprivileged, especially African Americans. As a teenager, he rode the bus to "Little Africa" in Richmond, where he preached on street corners, declaring that everyone was equal in the sight of God (Guinn 2017). In early stints at White churches, Jones didn't just sermonize equality; he invited African Americans to attend, which led to his ouster from two congregations. With the help of Marceline, he established two deliberately interracial churches in the segregated city of Indianapolis. Founded in 1954, Community Unity was a storefront church at the corner of Randolph and Hoyt Streets. When the small congregation of twenty-five elderly Black women and a smattering of Whites expanded and outgrew its location, Jim, Marceline, and Lynetta signed the articles of incorporation for Wings of Deliverance in April 1955. They borrowed money to purchase a church building on North New Jersey Street and the congregation relocated, becoming Peoples Temple a short time thereafter.

Pentecostal Christianity uses the term "Temple" frequently, and "Peoples" indicates the populist orientation of the movement (Hall 2004: 43–4).

Peoples Temple explicitly declared its commitment to integration. A newspaper ad from 1955 called it "The Miracle Church for All Groups, Or the One Human Race" ("Peoples Temple Ad" 1955). Another ad proclaimed that Peoples Temple was for all races and denominations, while yet another offered "lovely gifts" to the person who brings the most visitors to church. It also announced free fellowship meals at 12:00 noon and 5:00 p.m. ("Peoples Temple Ad" 1956a). The Temple did in fact "truly practice" charity, as its advertising claimed, providing a food pantry, offering free meals after church services, opening the Free Restaurant, establishing or purchasing care homes for the elderly, and engaging in local politics with members attending city council meetings.

The Joneses lived their integrationist message in a "rainbow family" proposed by Marceline (Guinn 2017). It comprised adopted daughter Agnes (White), Stephanie and Lew (Korean), Jim Jones Jr. (African American), and Stephan, their only biological child. Stephan was named after Stephanie, who died in an auto accident three weeks before his birth. Marceline reported having a vision in which Stephanie told her of another Korean child in need of adoption. When the Joneses learned from the adoption agency that Stephanie had a sister, they adopted her and named her Suzanne. Throughout the years, Jim and Marceline would gather many young adults to them who considered the two their adoptive parents.

The visibility of Jim Jones and his people in the community led to his appointment to direct the Indianapolis Human Rights Commission in January 1961. Typically an honorary rather than activist position, the directorship under Jones became highly visible. With the help of his diverse congregation, Jones successfully integrated a number of restaurants, persuaded White homeowners to welcome their new Black neighbors, ended segregation at the downtown movie theater, and generally brought racial discrimination to the forefront of public awareness – so much so that he and his family received threatening letters and telephone calls. The pressure aggravated an ulcer and caused an emotional breakdown, which sent Jim to the hospital in fall 1961. His doctor recommended a two-month leave of absence. After a brief trip to British Guiana (its spelling before independence in 1966), Jim was joined by his family in Hawaii for the balance of his convalescence (Guinn 2017: 110–11). They returned to Indianapolis and, shortly thereafter, Jim resigned from the Human Rights Commission.

Presumably in search of a new mission field, or possibly a place to relocate the Temple, or even a safe haven from nuclear attack, Jim and Marceline moved to Brazil in early January 1962 with their four youngest children. They left Peoples Temple in the hands of associates with the assumption that the church would continue to prosper and support them financially in their mission. Although accounts vary of the sojourn to Belo Horizonte and later to Rio de Janeiro (Thielmann with Merrill 1979; Reiterman with Jacobs 1982; Hougan 2003), most agree that the Jones family lived with and worked among the poorest of the poor. Jim himself declared that he raised "a pile of money" to buy food for the orphanages he supplied by having sex with an "ambassador's wife" (J. Jones 1977). Hearing reports both of dissension back in Indianapolis and of a drop-off in membership, however, Jim and his family returned to Indiana at the end of 1963.

The quest for greener and safer pastures continued and a few Temple members moved to northern California in 1964, where Jim visited them. Pleased with what he found, Jim guided some one hundred and forty followers, Black and White in roughly equal numbers, to Ukiah, California, in 1965. The relocation occurred for three primary reasons (Moore 2018a). First, Jim Jones's concern over nuclear war was sincere; if not, he could have moved to a major metropolitan area rather than an out-of-the-way rural region. Second, Jones had begun to reinvent himself as a prophet with divine gifts; this new identity might best be recognized by newcomers rather than old-timers. Third, the Brazil experience taught him that he needed to keep a tighter grip on the group. The migration therefore increased the dependence that followers had upon their leader by isolating them from their neighbors. In addition, the move allowed the focus to shift from Jesus Christ to Jim Jones (Moore 2018a: 23). Moreover, California was at the forefront of the struggle for racial justice (Harris & Waterman 2004), although that is not what minority Temple members discovered in conservative Redwood Valley. The group of migrants nevertheless attracted new members – some from Christ's Church of the Golden Rule, another communal group residing in the area; some from the local continuation high school, where Jim Jones taught; and some from the San Francisco Bay Area. Peoples Temple was growing again.

Redwood Valley

Although the Peoples Temple of the Disciples of Christ incorporated in California in 1965, it wasn't until 1969 that the Temple opened its own building in Redwood Valley, nine miles north of Ukiah. The Disciples of Christ, or Christian Church, identification was important, giving the once-independent apostolic church the imprimatur of a liberal mainline denomination. The Disciples accepted Peoples Temple into the denomination in 1960 and officially ordained Jim Jones in 1964, after he earned a degree from Butler University in Indiana. By November 1978, Peoples Temple contributed more money annually to the denomination than any other congregation.

But in 1969, the Temple was still finding its footing. It was in Redwood Valley that experiments in cooperative labor and communal living began. Once the church itself was built, additional facilities went up: a laundry, apartments, a print shop, a garage. Bay Area visitors, mostly White, found the message and the members of the Temple congenial and compelling. It was at this point in the Temple's history – the 1960s – that a number of young, White, college-educated adults joined the interracial working class members from Indiana (Maaga 1998: 10). They moved into the area and shared housing with others. Several worked for the social welfare department, helping people navigate the welfare system. They also directed them to the Temple for additional services. Others taught in the public school system, while still others worked at the local Masonite factory or the state hospital in Talmage. Newly arriving married couples took in foster children from the state or raised the children of Temple members in their homes in the Valley.

Inside the sanctuary, they listened to a message of socialist redemption and a critique of capitalism. Jim Jones excoriated the "Sky God" of traditional religion (FBI Audiotape Q1022 1973) and disparaged King James and his Bible, which justified enslaving Africans. "All of our trouble comes out of this," he exclaimed, patting the Bible (FBI Audiotape Q1019 1973). Jones also asserted that he was divine and in fact was the reincarnation of Jesus Christ (FBI Audiotape Q1024 1974). Members didn't just listen to sermons, however. They also participated in the practice of self-confession and punishment. Called "catharsis," the sessions required members to publicly admit their transgressions. Since insiders knew what was expected, most confessions were fabricated, such as "disclosing" their pedophilia, their homosexuality, or their sexual desire for Jim Jones. Others had a ring of truth, such as conceding that they not only went to a baseball game, but that they had bought a ticket with money that could have been given to the church (FBI Audiotape Q1021 1972). The sins included chewing gum, reading the newspaper during a church service, and not setting a good example for others. Catharsis bound people closer to each other within the circle of their so-called secrets, giving both Jones and the membership power over individuals (Moore 2022a). It also strengthened – or was intended to strengthen – the commitment to a socialist lifestyle in which the good of everyone eclipsed the welfare of the individual.

The face the Temple presented to the community, however, was far from radical. Members were helpful, good citizens who contributed to the community. But since many in the Temple were also Black living in largely White

Redwood Valley, attacks on members of color happened on the school grounds and in the streets. While these instances actually occurred, a more dramatic event did not. An assassination attempt on Jones's life in summer 1972 was contrived to elicit sympathy and awe in his followers. The point of the drama was clear. "From then on, it would be one hell of a fight," Stephan Jones said. "It would be a conflict – they would be constantly trying to snuff us out" (FBI Audiotape Q616 1978).

Redwood Valley was probably never intended as the last stop in the Temple's ascent. The same year that the Temple opened its newly built sanctuary there, members began making forays into San Francisco and Los Angeles. In 1972, the group bought two properties: it dedicated an old Christian Science church building at 1336 South Alvarado Street as the Los Angeles Temple and purchased a former Scottish Rite Temple at 1859 Geary in San Francisco. It also bought a large ranch in Redwood Valley to house mentally challenged young adults in a bucolic environment. Although the Temple settled in rural northern California, it was clear that it was heading for bigger things.

San Francisco and Los Angeles

A fleet of eleven Greyhound-sized buses took people from Redwood Valley to Temple services in San Francisco and Los Angeles on alternate Sundays, while the core group returned to Redwood Valley to work during the week. Staff were assigned to the new outposts and the congregations in both cities understandably came to surpass the membership and clout of their "mother church." The entry into urban environments was a natural outgrowth of the commitment to racial equality – a struggle that could only be lived out in cities with sizable populations of African Americans. In these new venues, the Temple could add elements of anticolonialism to its rhetoric and include participants in anticolonial movements on its guest lists. The clandestine socialism practiced in Redwood Valley became a very public internationalism in the cities.

The Los Angeles Temple operated along the lines of a traditional church. It was important to the movement because it served as its main source of revenue, raising $25,000 or more every weekend (Guinn 2017: 247). But Los Angeles was too big and too conservative for the Temple to make much of an impact. San Francisco, the city on a hill, was more conducive geographically, politically, and socially.

The Temple in San Francisco enlarged many of the basic services begun in Redwood Valley. Members developed programs to help poor people through the welfare system and committed themselves to communal living and housing, with perhaps one hundred members donating their entire paycheck in exchange for room, board, healthcare coverage, and modest expenses. Some simply shared housing owned by the Temple itself. Members served their own, assisting those who were incarcerated (or, more frequently, whose relatives were incarcerated), providing healthcare services to the elderly, and offering free legal advice on evictions, divorces, and, on occasion, criminal cases. They also helped the wider community by participating in coalition movements and, to a limited extent, local politics.

On the last day of 1976, Jim Jones confided to his top aide, Tim Stoen, "It was our year of ascendancy" (Guinn 2017: 338). The year 1976 did indeed see the rise of a noticeable and activist Temple, and new star power for its leader. Notable VIPs, including Los Angeles mayor Tom Bradley, San Francisco district attorney Joseph Freitas, Communist Party member Angela Davis, and California lieutenant governor Mervyn Dymally, shared the stage with Jones at the joint Peoples Temple–Nation of Islam "spiritual jubilee" held that May. The Temple and, more visibly, its leader took public stands with other Black leaders in support of amnesty for Black Panther Party leader Eldridge Cleaver. Jones appeared with United Methodist celebrity minister Cecil Williams of Glide Memorial Church at a rally protesting the US Supreme Court decision that preferential treatment in school admissions based on minority status was unconstitutional. Backed by the "people power" of the Temple, Jones grew in status. He frequently met with San Francisco County leaders and Democratic decision-makers in spring 1976, but he rejected the first political prize offered to him when he spurned a place on the Human Rights Commission. It wasn't until October that he was nominated to and accepted an appointment to the County Housing Authority. He was elevated to chair a few months later.

The icing on the cake was Jones's brief meeting with Walter Mondale on the vice presidential candidate's private jet in October. According to Temple diarist Edith Roller, Jones told the congregation privately that he talked to Mondale about Guyana and the problem of the United States squeezing the "socialist country out of existence" (Roller 1976c). Other signs of growing political influence included the California State Senate's adoption of a resolution commending Jim Jones and his group. The discovery of individuals using electronic surveillance outside the Temple to monitor a speech given by Unita Blackwell – the recently elected mayor of Mayersville, Mississippi, and the first African American ever to be elected mayor in that state – seemed to affirm the prominence of the Temple: it was worth spying on.

In hindsight, 1976 was indeed the culmination of the two-decades-long odyssey of Peoples Temple, from its Midwestern origins to San Francisco, where the church achieved esteem, respectability, and fame. But 1976 was also the apex. Critics had already begun to defect. Corporal punishments within the inner circle of the Temple and amongst the most trusted members of the congregation intensified. Jim Jones became increasingly dependent on drugs.

Behind closed doors, a hierarchical leadership structure orbited around Jim Jones. An inner circle that included Marceline Jones, several White women administrators (some of whom were his mistresses), and a few White male associates comprised the next level, protecting the leader and implementing his orders. The Planning Commission (PC) made up the third level. Begun in Redwood Valley, the PC increased in size and stature in San Francisco. Membership grew from about thirty-seven in 1973 to roughly one hundred by 1977; the majority of those in positions of responsibility, such as finance, counseling, or public relations, were White (Moore 2018a: 36). The PC made decisions about policy and planning, but also served as the locus for the most severe punishments, including sexual shaming and abuse. Jones's apparent obsession with sex and his claim to superlative powers, coupled with the obvious racial disparity in leadership, provoked the departure of eight young adults in 1973. They wrote an eleven-page heartfelt letter to their leader, criticizing "staff," as Temple leaders were called. They complained of the preoccupation with sexual matters, the racism inherent in staff promotions, and the lack of revolutionary commitment, pointing out the many instances of double standards and hypocrisy along the way ("The Eight Revolutionaries" 1973).

Nineteen seventy-three was also the year that the Temple board of directors passed a resolution to establish an agricultural mission in Guyana ("Resolution to Establish Agricultural Mission" 1973). Early the next year, a group of pioneers traveled to the Northwest District of Guyana to begin developing the project: clearing out jungle, excavating roads, and constructing buildings. Activity commenced even before the Temple signed a lease for 3,852 acres with the government of Guyana ("Guyana Land Lease" 1976), although Temple leaders and Guyana officials had been in negotiations for two years. Peoples Temple would gain a haven for its members outside the United States and Guyana would settle a group of Americans near its disputed border with Venezuela. It seemed to be a win-win situation for all parties.

Guyana

Getting a clear understanding of life in Jonestown depends upon the sources used. The journals of Edith Roller, who lived and died in Jonestown, paint one picture (Roller 2013). Memoirs by Hyacinth Thrash, Leslie Wagner-Wilson, Laura Johnston Kohl, and Eugene Smith depict another (Thrash 1995; Wagner-Wilson 2008; Kohl 2010; Smith 2021), and that of Deborah Layton something else entirely (D. Layton 1998). The migration to Guyana created new challenges for the organization, most especially the difficulties inherent to creating an entire agricultural village from scratch. Each month presented different opportunities and complications for those living and working in Guyana. Life in Jonestown was radically different in summer 1976, for example, when those building the community had high hopes, than it was in summer 1978, when the situation began to deteriorate rapidly.

"In the early days of Jonestown, everybody was enthusiastic, full of hope for a new beginning" (P. Blakey 2018). Those involved in the planning, construction, and development of the project envisioned a new society free of poverty, drugs, and violence and lacking the evils of racism, sexism, and ageism. They saw themselves as a vanguard, as one survivor wrote, with the goal of creating "a community that allowed my children – and my children's children – to grow up in a more peaceful, humane, and caring society that eventually might *become* a 'Utopia'" (T. Carter 2008). Others saw the commune as heaven on earth. But with the rapid influx of immigrants from the United States in 1977, the small settlement was overwhelmed with the myriad issues that would require immediate attention in any small town: sanitation, roads, potable water, food procurement, housing, education, site beautification, and all of the other services we take for granted. Despite the overflowing dorms and cottages, most residents retained their good spirits until fears of a conspiracy against the group generated concerns about the community's security. A siege mentality emerged.

Beginning in 1977, a band of former members and families of Jonestown residents organized the Concerned Relatives to bring their fears to public attention. They described the abuse that occurred within the Temple and alleged that members murdered people attempting to leave (McGehee 2013c). The Concerned Relatives successfully generated media coverage and government attention in a variety of ways. Their efforts coalesced most powerfully in the person of Leo J. Ryan, a California congressman. A news story on the accidental death of Robert Houston, son of a good friend and constituent of Ryan, had already captured his attention. Throughout 1978, the Concerned Relatives contacted their congressional representatives, but Ryan was the only one willing to launch an investigation into Peoples Temple. News accounts that described a child custody suit filed by former members Grace and Tim Stoen, personal visits with the Stoens, and ongoing lobbying by Concerned Relatives increased his commitment. In early September, Ryan began to make plans for a visit to Jonestown with formal if reluctant support from his colleagues in Congress. On the first of November, he sent a telegram to Jim Jones announcing his intent to visit the community. Jonestown residents adopted a resolution and signed a petition dated November 9 protesting Ryan's visit. Four days later, they issued a four-page press release explaining their objections.

Against the advice of US State Department officials, Ryan encouraged members of the Concerned Relatives and reporters to join him in Guyana. Nine journalists accompanied Ryan's party to Jonestown (although one was denied entrance into the settlement), but only four of the fourteen Concerned Relatives who'd traveled to Guyana went with the congressman. Temple leaders, including Marceline, persuaded Jim to let Ryan's contingent into Jonestown on November 17, and on this first encounter relations were cordial. But the next day, reporters were more inquisitive and aggressive as it became apparent that some residents wanted to leave Jonestown. A man with a knife attacked Ryan but was disarmed. The congressman and his aides rounded up the few wishing to leave – fifteen in all, plus one man pretending to be a defector – in a chaotic scene of families being torn apart.

Two planes were waiting as the group arrived at the Port Kaituma airstrip when a dozen young men from Jonestown pulled up in a tractor-drawn trailer. They announced, "All Guyanese clear the airport," waving the locals away (James 2020). They then opened fire on those arriving from Jonestown, targeting the congressman and the members of the press. Five individuals died in the attack: Congressman Ryan, reporter Don Harris, cameraman Bob Brown, photographer Greg Robinson, and Jonestown defector Patricia Parks. Meanwhile, Larry Layton, who posed as a defector, opened fire in one of the planes he and actual defectors had boarded. He was disarmed, but not before wounding two individuals.

Back in Jonestown, the residents gathered in the central pavilion, where Jim Jones told them it was the end and now was the time to lay down their lives. Only a single person, Christine Miller, seemed to question the decision, according to a tape made during the proceedings (FBI Audiotape Q042 1978). Jones warned of an impending attack on the community with the prospect of children being tortured or enslaved. Ostensibly to prevent that inevitability, the children would be the first to die. One man remarked on this:

> And the way the children are laying there now, I'd rather see them lay like that than to see them have to die like the Jews did [in concentration camps]. ... Because, like Dad said, when they come in, what they're gonna do to our children – they're gonna massacre our children. (FBI Audiotape Q042 1978)

Many, if not most, of the children were murdered with a cyanide-laced punch squirted into their mouths with a needleless syringe. An unknown number of adults were possibly injected with hypodermic needles and still others simply drank a cup of poison after administering it to their children. Only two individuals were shot in Jonestown: Jim Jones and the author's sister Ann Elizabeth Moore – three individuals, if we count Mr. Muggs, the pet chimpanzee.

Dozens of books and articles supplement this spare account of the events leading to the deaths in Jonestown, although some are more accurate or trustworthy than others (e.g., Reiterman with Jacobs 1982; Hall 2004; Guinn 2017; Moore 2018a). Much of the history of Peoples Temple is contested, especially the actions that occurred on the last day and the immediate aftermath. The sections that follow go into some of these debates in greater detail. No amount of analysis, however, can redress the loss of human life on November 18, 1978. Nor should it.

2 The Religions of Peoples Temple

In the wake of the mass deaths at the hands of a group that presented itself as a Christian church, religious leaders and groups sought to distance themselves from Peoples Temple. The head of Campus Crusade for Christ was concerned that the news media might mistake legitimate Christian groups for cults like Peoples Temple (Rose 1979: 188). Black church leaders agreed that Peoples Temple should not be thought of as a "Black Church" (Moore 2018a: 115). Jonestown was simply one more example of the way in which Whites inflicted suffering upon Blacks. After Jonestown, "People's [*sic*] Temple was no longer considered part of … the universal church" (Rose 1979: 15). But a few voices were raised early on that expressed sympathy for the victims and sorrow for the loss of the community. The Reverend Muhammed Isaiah Kenyatta's reflections, published in 1979, praised the communalism of the "band of Christian pilgrims" and noted the irony of the Temple's flight to the Third World (Kenyatta 2004 [1979]: 161). Another Black pastor and scholar, Archie Smith Jr., echoed Kenyatta's sentiments. "It will be important to remember the positive and heroic things done by Peoples Temple which somewhere, somehow need to be continued" (A. Smith 2004: 53). In the immediate aftermath, however, Kenyatta and Smith's calls for repentance and renewal, for self-criticism and reflection, were minority reports. It took more than twenty-five years for one scholar to put Peoples Temple back into the interpretive framework of Christianity. Religious studies scholar Kristian Klippenstein argued that traditional Christian doctrines of sin and salvation were at work within the Temple, although redemption was interpreted as deliverance from the social injustices inherent in capitalism, hypocritical Christianity, and obscurity in life (Klippenstein 2009).

It is understandable that Peoples Temple would warrant criticism given the accounts of internal abuses and its violent ending. Religious studies scholar Holly Folk captured the difficulty of identifying the theology of the group:

> Shifts in beliefs over time, different perspectives of Temple members, and the fact that Jones himself made conflicting and dissembling statements about his beliefs mean that there is no single perspective that should be regarded as definitive. (Folk 2018: 17)

Folk maintained that Peoples Temple manifested "experiential pluralism" – that is, "the movement was intrinsically heterogeneous" (Folk 2018: 19). The Temple seemed to embrace different identities at different times in its existence. Undoubtedly, individuals within the movement had a primary ideological identification, with older members likely remaining Christians to the very end. Others seemed to abandon the beliefs of their childhood in favor of worldviews they found more meaningful, such as commitment to the alleviation of social problems or participation in making revolutionary change.

At the same time, the racism that pervaded the organization makes the assertion that Peoples Temple was a Black religion problematic if not inaccurate. Despite Jones's professed and even sincere empathy for the suffering and disenfranchisement of African Americans, his actions indicated the ongoing influence of racist thinking – from his choices of staff, to selections of lovers, to commitments to social issues. While Anthony Pinn observed that social movements should not be dismissed on the basis of the misdeeds or indiscretions of their leaders (Pinn 2004: 10), it remains troubling that the hierarchy of the group was largely White.

Nevertheless, the Temple retained many elements of Black religion, which is why African Americans felt comfortable in a church led by a White pastor. Eric Lincoln and Lawrence Mamiya noted that "religion is expressed in cultural forms like music and song, styles and content of preaching, and modes of worship" (Lincoln & Mamiya 2003: 7). In all of these respects the Temple reflected what they called the "black sacred cosmos." It therefore seems preferable to locate the religions of Peoples Temple under the umbrella of Black religion rather than strictly inside or outside Christianity. Black religion is "an elemental category of religious experience that relates to the Black Church but also to all other modalities of religious expression in African American communities" (Pinn 2004: 14). Pinn's expansive definition of Black religion serves to illuminate the fullness of belief systems in Peoples Temple, namely Pentecostal Christianity, New Thought, liberal Protestantism, and Humanism. An overarching theology of martyrdom, however, eventually superseded all belief systems held by Temple members.

The Pentecostal Church in the Temple

Although accounts of the origins of Pentecostalism vary, it is certain that the "intense enthusiasm and the open display of emotions and feelings exhibited by the worshiper" have their origins in the religiosity practiced by enslaved Africans in the United States (Lincoln & Mamiya 2003: 5). Pentecostalists speak in tongues, adopt an experiential and exuberant worship style, and emphasize physical and spiritual healing. They believe in submission to the Holy Spirit, the literal truth of the Bible, and the possibility of personal perfection. Religious elites once viewed Pentecostalism along with fundamentalism as a religion of the lower classes, and to a limited extent this was true in the early twentieth century. Mainline or mainstream Protestants generally required an educated clergy who could interpret scripture in accordance with church tradition and seminary training. In contrast, Pentecostal Christians ordained those who demonstrated the gift of prophecy, the power of spiritual discernment, and the manifestation of a Spirit-filled life. Formal training might come later if at all. (These differences are not quite as sharp in the twenty-first century as they were in the twentieth.)

In the early 1950s, while serving as a volunteer student pastor at Somerset Methodist Church in Indianapolis, Jim Jones was also roaming the Midwest revival circuit, learning the craft of preaching, prophesying, and healing. Although the social creed of the Methodist Church appealed to him, the kinetic warmth of worship along with his own charismatic gifts and desire for free rein, theologically speaking, took him into Pentecostalism. By various accounts, Jones was a popular preacher and faith healer in Midwestern revivalism (Hall 2004; Guinn 2017; M. Jones n.d.[a]. and n.d.[b]). He attracted the attention of William Branham (1909–65), one of several popular revivalists credited with launching the postwar Healing Revival. Many evangelists were part of this movement, including Billy Graham and Oral Roberts, but Branham was noted for focusing on a "'supernatural' ministry of healings, prophecies, and other paranormal phenomena" (Melton 2003: 87). It was therefore something of a coup for Peoples Temple to host William Branham and other Pentecostal luminaries at a revival in June 1956 and to sponsor a second in 1957. Yet the majority of attendees came from Peoples Temple and that majority was African American (Guinn 2017: 82).

It is clear that Branham-style religion, known as Deliverance Pentecostalism, influenced Jones (Collins 2018). A few months before the 1956 revival, he was ordained in the Independent Assemblies of God. Its practices – such as relying on present-day apostles and emphasizing the importance of the laying on of hands – were condemned by the original Assemblies of God (Melton 2003: 88).

Both Jones and Branham veered into heresy when they intimated that they were manifesting God's "Spoken Word" with their own oracles. "That's what I am," Jones announced to the Los Angeles congregation in 1974. "The Word. The Spoken Word. *The Living Word*" (FBI Audiotape Q612 1974).

In their roles as "manifested sons of God," William Branham and Jim Jones were also prophets of both the quotidian and the cosmic. They predicted misfortune, accidents, illness, and other catastrophes individuals might experience in order to prevent their occurrence. Calling people out by name and even by street address – a stratagem Jones learned from Branham – Jones warned his followers of car problems, prostate issues, and ruthless landlords. But Branham and Jones shared a larger agenda. Branham had a distinct doomsday expectation framed within the Cold War context of the battle with godless communism. Although Jones seemed to embrace communism, at least secretly, he too expected a final reckoning through atomic war. Indeed, his conviction that some sort of catastrophic event – whether military or political – was imminent seemed to drive the Temple's migrations from one place to the next.

Branham and Jones shared a commitment to integration as well, though modestly for the former and wholeheartedly for the latter. The postwar Healing Revival was one of the few places where integrated worship could be found in the 1940s and 1950s. "From the beginning, the revival, supported largely by poor whites, bypassed many of the customs of racial prejudice" (Harrell 1975: 98). A few revivalists encouraged mixed audiences with integrated seating in their evangelistic ministries and Jones was no exception. Newspaper ads highlighted the interracial elements of the church. An ad from 1956 bore the headline: "Peoples Temple. Interracial–Interdenominational." To make sure the message was clear, the tag line at the bottom stated: "We Teach and Practice complete integration in the family, church and vocational fields" ("Peoples Temple Ad" 1956b).

Other advertisements promised a "miracle healing service" because healings became a central element of Jim Jones's ministry. Even as he opened his first storefront church in Indianapolis, he honed his healing skills at revivals throughout the Midwest. He began by relying on his own intuitions but soon learned the tricks of the healing trade – eavesdropping on conversations as audiences gathered outside revival tents, taking names and addresses for future contact, and, eventually, producing solid evidence of cancers that had been vomited up.

Yet some Temple members were convinced that they experienced genuine healing. After a doctor in Indianapolis told Hyacinth Thrash that she had breast cancer, Jim Jones and several other church members laid hands on her. Not only did the lump disappear, but "seven doctors at St. Vincent hospital examined [her], and the tumor was gone" (Thrash 1995: 66). While Don Beck admitted that many healings in California were fraudulent, "the fact remains, [Jim Jones] had a gift" (Beck 2005a). Beck went on to describe four personal instances of healing – including the verified restoration of hearing to his five-year-old son. "That's why I can't dismiss the healings out of hand" (Beck 2005a). Dozens of statements written by Jonestown residents testify to the ways in which Jim Jones healed them – from curing constipation and reducing blood sugar to eliminating the need for eyeglasses. Perhaps most important, members believed that they had been healed.

Whereas other faith healing ministries neglected traditional medicine, Temple publicity stressed the need for ordinary healthcare treatment. "We do NOT oppose medical science," proclaimed one ad from the 1950s ("Peoples Temple Ad" 1956c, original typography). "THIS SANE SPIRITUAL HEALING MINISTRY IN NO WAY OPPOSES MEDICAL SCIENCE, for all good things come down from above," according to *The Living Word* in the 1970s (1972: 23, original typography). The fact that the Temple administered free tests for sickle cell anemia, a disease that targets African Americans, in San Francisco and regularly took blood pressure readings from senior citizens in San Francisco and Jonestown seemed to attest to the importance of sound medical treatment. Although reports from Jonestown assert that Jones restored a severed hand, the community also had a health clinic to treat athlete's foot, heart disease, and urinary tract infections.

Even in its liberal Protestant manifestation, Peoples Temple continued to follow "the model of the emotionally expressive Pentecostal tradition" (Harrison 2004: 129). The largely Black congregation welcomed the call-and-response style of exhortation and engaged format of worship. It both anticipated and expected that music would undergird the entire worship service. Jim Jones, a White man, provided a Black congregation exactly what they wanted:

> a highly participatory, celebratory, dynamic form of expository preaching, along with a message that sharply criticized the Christian church's hypocrisy and complicity in perpetuating the oppression of the poor, the weak, and the racially and ethnically marginalized segments of society.
>
> (Harrison 2004: 135)

Thus the Temple's origins within American Pentecostalism point to one of Pinn's "modalities" of Black religion. Pentecostal style continued to inform the performance of worship, if not the actual content, throughout the Temple's existence.

New Thought in the Temple

Historian Adam Morris carefully traced a possible and plausible New Thought genealogy for Jim Jones – who credited his conversations with "messengers" in order to effect healings – to the reading he may have done of Edgar Cayce (1877–1947), Andrew Jackson Davis (1826–1910), and others (Morris 2018). One New Thought theme that permeated the sermons of Jim Jones was, "For as he thinketh within himself, so is he" (Proverbs 27:3), more often simply paraphrased, "As a man thinketh, so he is" (FBI Audiotape Q945 1977; FBI Audiotape Q974 1973; FBI Audiotape Q1055-2 1966, among others). The importance of mind over matter to realize ultimate truths such as radical equality and the divinity within haunted Jones's sermons. An unambiguous New Thought connection, however, and one that directly linked the Temple to Black religious traditions was the Peace Mission of Father Divine.

Born as George Baker (1877–1965) to formerly enslaved parents, Father Divine established a popular and controversial interracial movement called the Peace Mission in the 1920s. The diminutive Black man explicitly asserted that he was God, and his disciples wholeheartedly believed it. His own claims to divinity notwithstanding, Divine also taught that God exists within all people and sought to make this a material reality for his followers in elaborate "Heavenly Banquets" that featured ten, twenty, and thirty courses of food (Griffith 2001). Divine's heyday came during the Great Depression, when from Harlem he oversaw hundreds of small businesses, invested in profitable real estate ventures, and provided free and low-cost meals and inexpensive lodging for his followers. By the 1950s, however, membership in the Peace Mission had dwindled considerably, and the leader and his second wife lived in seclusion on an estate outside of Philadelphia.

Jones's theological debt to Father Divine and the Peace Mission has been discussed extensively (Reiterman with Jacobs 1982; Hall 2004; Guinn 2017), and most especially by a writer under the pseudonym E. Black (Black 2012, 2014, 2015). It seems likely that Jones learned of the Peace Mission from the 1953 book *Father Divine, Holy Husband* since sociologist Sara Harris's ethnographic account was found in his personal library (Wooden 1981: 59). His description of the Peace Mission used Harris's own language (J. Jones 1959). Jones and his wife, Marceline, first visited Father Divine in late 1956 and continued to make visits throughout the late 1950s (Guinn 2017). In one of the few works he personally authored, Jones described a visit (probably a composite of several visits) in *Pastor Jones Meets Rev. M. J. Divine: Better Known As Father Divine* (J. Jones 1959).

Although Jones criticized the deification of Divine, he also praised the "mutual cooperation and complete sanctification" he witnessed at one of the Heavenly Banquets (J. Jones 1959: 8). He especially appreciated "the flower garden of integration [that] is a perfect reality in all Peace Mission churches throughout the world" (J. Jones 1959: 11). Thus, while he was sharing the stage with Christian evangelist William Branham, who stated that he was The Message, The Spoken Word, and a Manifested Son of God, Jones was also visiting Father Divine, whose followers called him God in a body and who himself said that he was God. It might appear difficult to sort out who had the greater influence on Jones were it not for Father Divine's clear commitment to interracial living and his establishment of a communal empire. Branham's itinerant ministry, although profitable, was not what Jones was looking for.

In fact, it may have been the success of Father Divine's communal enterprise, rather than the fear of nuclear war, that drove Jones and the Temple to California. In rural Redwood Valley he could replicate the Peace Mission's successful agricultural endeavors in Upstate New York. Yet he still dreamed of leading a group the size and scope of the Peace Mission. After the death of Father Divine, Jones attempted to persuade Mother Divine in 1971 that he was Divine's reincarnation and should head the movement (Reiterman with Jacobs 1982: 139–40). Rebuffed, he returned to California and began to have his followers call him Father and Marceline, Mother. A year later, he started ministries in San Francisco and Los Angeles.

Peoples Temple therefore embodied a second modality of Black religion in its explicit and implicit adoption of tenets of New Thought. Black religion in America is frequently equated with the Black Church, a view that neglects African-derived beliefs in conjure, hoodoo, magic, and spiritual healing (Chireau 2003). It also ignores the history of Black leadership of New Thought movements and the acceptance of metaphysical principles by ordinary African Americans. A partial list of nineteenth-century Black contributors to New Thought metaphysics comprised Mother Leafy Anderson, the National Colored Spiritualist Association, Prince Hall Masonry, Pascal Beverly Randolph, and Sojourner Truth (Albanese 2007: 601). In the twentieth century, prominent practitioners included Marcus Garvey, Sarah Flowers, and J. Arthur Twyne, as well as Father Divine.

Most members of the Temple accepted several principles of New Thought – the divine within, the unity of all religions, the power of the mind, the realization of heaven on earth, reincarnation, and other teachings. Several people belonged to New Thought religious groups such as Unity School of Christianity either before they joined the Temple or after they left. Christ's Church of the Golden Rule, a metaphysical community that offered the original meeting space for

Peoples Temple in Redwood Valley, supplied converts to the group. The use of prayer cloths, photographs of Jim Jones, and other religious paraphernalia indicates ongoing belief in the thaumaturgical powers of things imbued with sacred power – in other words, hoodoo. Thus, New Thought, though often considered a White phenomenon, contributed to the Black religious profile of Peoples Temple.

The Liberal Protestant Church in the Temple

In Indianapolis, the Temple boasted of being "interdenominational," although it also retained the "apostolic" descriptor in advertisements. If William Branham began to condemn denominationalism as Revelation's mark of the beast (Weaver 1987), Jim Jones saw the benefits of affiliation with a denomination: recognition, legitimacy, and at times financial assistance. The Disciples of Christ, a liberal mainline denomination, has a reputation for commitment to social justice and insistence on congregational independence. It helped that the Disciples were headquartered in Indianapolis and that Jones became acquainted with Barton Hunter, a Disciples official. With little prompting from Hunter, the Temple congregation voted to join the Disciples and set out a sign announcing "Peoples Temple Christian Church Full Gospel" (Hall 2004: 52–3). The formal approval process took longer, and when the church achieved full status in 1960, it was with the proviso that Jones must earn a college degree to receive ordination. He did so and was ordained four years later. (Guinn [2017: 96–7] provides a slightly different account of the process of affiliation with the Disciples.)

The Disciples of Christ were in many ways the perfect body for Peoples Temple to join since they have "no creed but Christ," a belief tested only by affirming that "Jesus is the Christ, the son of the living God" (Stroup 2007). This is a credo many Temple members could adopt. The Disciples also elevate congregational independence and decision-making above that of a national or international polity. "The only authority to which a Christian should be subject," according to Disciples thought, "is the people in the congregation to which he belongs" (Stroup 2007). The benefits of such congregational liberty are clear. But so are the dangers. Lacking oversight by outsider observers, an independent congregation can depart from traditional Christian teachings with no one noticing. This is exactly what happened in Peoples Temple.

The Bible-based preaching that attracted African Americans and Whites in the 1950s and 1960s was replaced by jeremiads against the Bible as an instrument of oppression. A sermon from 1972 attacked King James, the one authorizing an English translation of the Bible, "who took the first ship – [the] Good

Figure 3 Woman in Los Angeles congregation of Peoples Temple, date unknown. Courtesy of the Special Collections and University Archives, San Diego State University Library

Ship Jesus – [and] brought back Blacks in chains, and he murdered people all over the whole world" (FBI Audiotape Q1035 1972). In this sermon and others, Jones pointed out all the instances in which the Bible advocates violence, slavery, and subjugation of women. He authored a pamphlet titled "The Letter Killeth," typewritten sheets that list all of the errors, absurdities, atrocities, and inconsistencies in the Bible, though it also begins by noting the "great truths of the Bible" (J. Jones n.d.).

The theological emphasis in the Temple shifted from the personal holiness valorized in Pentecostal tradition to the social holiness, or social gospel, stressed in liberal Protestantism. "The righting of an oppressive, unjust social system has always been the expectation expressed through the religion of African Americans in the midst of their experience" (Harrison 2004: 128). Service programs expanded in the urban centers of San Francisco and Los Angeles and members engaged in coalition movements for racial equality. Jones shared the pulpit with guest speakers from a range of progressive causes, including civil rights, Native American rights, and gay rights. Representatives from national liberation movements from around the world also related their experiences to the congregation at lectures and programs hosted by the Temple. "Rev. Jones doesn't disallow the spiritual side of the church by any means," according to a 1976 Temple press release. "But the practical emphasis gained more thrust from the belief in Peoples Temple that the highest worship of God or Deity is service to one's fellow man" ("Press Release" 1976).

Humanism in the Temple

The criticism of the Bible, coupled with an emphasis on the practice of Christianity rather than the beliefs of Christianity, points to elements of Humanism within the Temple. Certainly a Humanist outlook was evident in the protest letter written by the "Eight Revolutionaries" who left in 1973 criticizing the apparent racism of staff selections in the organization.

> We want it known by you and staff that we don't believe in religion, we don't believe in God, we don't believe in reincarnation, we don't believe in impossible. We are not concerned with the beginning, the end or the hereafter. We are only concerned about today. ("The Eight Revolutionaries" 1973)

Religion historian David Chidester's phenomenological analysis of the Temple also suggested a turn toward Humanism in the quest for a socialist utopia. In one sermon, Jones complained that "We mine harbors, we blow up little babies this last week, and we ... don't want to do anything to build a better world and make the kingdom of heaven a reality here on earth, to build an apostolic socialism as it was on the day of the New Testament" (FBI Audiotape Q1059-2 1972). Chidester viewed Jones's obscenities and outrages as one way the preacher tried to cut through the artifice and pretensions of traditional Christianity (Chidester 2003: xiii).

A type of theistic Humanism seemed to be present in Temple theology. Jones preached that true love, the kind that uplifts, is apostolic sharing – that is, socialism. The New Testament book of Acts of the Apostles described the practice of early Christians to distribute resources among themselves as needed (Acts 2:44–45 and 4:32–35). Moreover, the biblical Sky God who allowed injustice to reign on earth was not the genuine God. Divine, or apostolic, socialism was the principle by which all should live. "See, socialism is love. Love is God. God is socialism. Draw close and hug your neighbor close to you," Jones exhorted the congregation in 1973 (FBI Audiotape Q1059-3 1973). Not only was Jim Jones God Almighty, as he frequently declared, but so too were the members of the Temple (e.g., FBI Audiotape Q1055-1 1975). "Ye are all gods," Jones repeatedly said, quoting Jesus in the Gospel of John (10:31–34). Although some Temple worship services encouraged the veneration of Jim Jones, others focused on commitment to the Cause, namely the apostolic community of first-century Christianity and the socialist society of twentieth-century America.

This explains why the needs of the group were privileged over those of the individual. Temple members and leaders alike espoused this view. The Peoples Temple Songbook, a compilation of popular songs used in Temple services, included one titled "Brotherhood Is Our Religion" with the lyrics:

> Brotherhood is our religion; For democracy we stand;
> We love everybody; We need every hand.
> It's based on the constitution and it certainly is God's command;
> These are the rights we adore: Liberty, Fraternity, Equality for all
> These are the rights we stand for! ("Peoples Temple Songbook" n.d.)

Another example of the centrality of the Humanistic worldview appears in a letter written by the author's sister Annie Moore about the relevance of faith healings to the real goal: brotherhood. "That's just a sideline so that we will know that working for true brotherhood is the right thing to do" (Moore 1986: 84).

By the time one thousand people were living in Jonestown, Pentecostalism, New Thought, and liberal Protestantism had fallen away, leaving atheistic Humanism as the dominant ideological commitment. Community meetings, civil defense drills, and educational programs replaced sermons and worship. Jim Jones shifted from claiming to behave like an atheist (FBI Audiotape Q932 1972) to asserting that he had been an atheist since childhood (J. Jones 1977). In preparation for a visit from Soviet dignitaries in October 1978, he reminded the community that "we are atheists, as all dialectical materialists are" (FBI Audiotape Q887 1978).

African Americans have a long but little-known tradition of Humanism (Pinn 2001). Indeed, for all of the doctrinaire rhetoric espoused in Jonestown and the repeated testing in communist terminology, most residents were, theologically at any rate, humanists. At various meetings and at stress-filled "White Nights" – occasions in which members of the community prepared to withstand what they believed would be a violent attack – residents testified to their commitment to each other and to socialism. Their ultimate concern was preservation of the community, even to the point of death (Wessinger 2000: 45, 48). Communal solidarity, based in Humanism rather than other spiritual traditions, became the primary religion in Jonestown.

The Theology of Martyrdom

Despite the diversity of religious perspectives held by Temple members, two threads wove them all together. The theology of apostolic socialism reflects the conviction that ultimate divinity existed in love lived out concretely. It was not an abstract commitment to the Cause – although that was present as well – but rather day-to-day living together with all its minor disputes and petty irritations. Deep generosity of spirit also characterized apostolic socialism as Jonestown residents experienced it.

At the same time a type of apocalyptic socialism defined the group as well. This came from the conviction that life for African Americans under capitalism could never be redeemed apart from a violent, world-shattering transformation. In this respect Peoples Temple was a catastrophic millennial group (Wessinger 2000) maintaining a pessimistic outlook about humans and society. With a radically dualistic perspective that divided the world between good and evil, "us and them," catastrophic millennialists may resort to violence in order to achieve their goal of a creating a new society on earth (Wessinger 2011). This is not always the case, however, for, as Hall observed, Peoples Temple functioned as both an apocalyptic warring sect and as an otherworldly sect (Hall 2004). It was a warring sect in its this-worldly battle for survival against its cultural opponents – relatives, the news media, and government actors. It was other-worldly, however, in its attempt to migrate to a location far from an oppressive capitalistic society and, when that failed, its transition to a supernatural or heavenly sanctuary (Hall 2004: 298–9).

A theology of martyrdom emerged from the combination of apostolic social-ism and its emphasis on solidarity with apocalyptic socialism and its bleak view of both the present and the future. Even before the move to Guyana, an ideology of self-sacrifice pervaded Temple teachings. Guest speakers featured at the San Francisco Temple described the tortures they endured for liberation, and graphic films displayed gross abuses. Teri Buford reported that Jim Jones and another resident of Jonestown pressed a hot spoon against her stomach to see if she could stand the pain (McGehee 2018). As early as 1973, the eight revolutionary defectors stated that "We feel that you came to the people giving them the greatest reason to live, the greatest reason to die, the greatest reason to fight – socialism" ("The Eight Revolutionaries" 1973). The reality of martyrdom crystallized in Jonestown, where adults and adolescents alike frequently con-fessed at community meetings their willingness to die for the Cause. They also wrote notes to Jim Jones that detailed their plans for resistance and death. "Many, perhaps most, of the adult participants understood the Jonestown mass suicide as a redemptive act." They saw it as the only way to rescue "a human identity from dehumanization under the capitalist, racist, and fascist oppression they associated with America" (Chidester 2003: xviii). In a single event, the residents of Jonestown ritually purified themselves and society, released themselves from suffering, gained revenge against their enemies, and signaled their absolute faith in the ultimate victory of revolution (Chidester 2003: 133–5).

3 The Politics of Peoples Temple

A little more than a decade after the Jonestown tragedy, the Berlin Wall fell. The collapse of the Soviet Union was not far behind. But for almost forty-five years, the battle for hearts and minds – the communist/totalitarian way or the capitalist/libertarian way – decisively influenced both domestic and international politics in the United States. At home, a civil rights movement began in the 1950s in order to end the structural racism that existed across the nation. African Americans militantly yet peaceably resisted the de facto and de jure segregation present in schools, housing, employment, and public services. The vast majority of those joining the struggle seeking justice and equality came directly from Black churches, although a few activists were members of the Communist Party. Even though McCarthyism was condemned in the 1950s, a suspicion of communist infiltrators remained and participants of many political movements – civil rights, antiwar, anticolonial – were denounced as communists. Abroad, the United States attempted to suppress nationalist uprisings in Africa and Asia. The nation's support for right-wing dictatorships around the world reflected this stance.

It is impossible to consider Peoples Temple or its politics apart from the Cold War – the struggle for global supremacy between the United States and the Union of Soviet Socialist Republics waged from the end of World War II until the fall of the Berlin Wall in 1989. From their transformation as bourgeois churchgoers into a revolutionary vanguard, to their immigration to the Cooperative Republic of Guyana, Temple members saw themselves engaged in a life-and-death struggle against the evils of capitalism. Their fight required reeducation through stringent behavior modification methods, secrecy and lying to outsiders, and, ultimately, complete removal from a hopelessly corrupt world. Although their enemies did not see themselves within the framework of Cold War politics, clearly Jonestown residents regarded them as agents of capitalism, fascism, and a racist society. Moreover, within the context of anticultism in the 1970s, accusations of brainwashing certainly comprised part of the rhetorical tool kit used by anticommunists and anticultists alike, as evidenced in FBI memoranda summarizing agents' interviews with returning survivors and cult experts. A competing rhetoric of revolution and resistance leading to martyrdom, however, also made up the conflict between the Temple and its cultural opponents, who consisted of family members, the news media, and government agencies.

Thus, we find evidence of Holly Folk's "experiential pluralism" not only in the religious beliefs of Peoples Temple members but also in their political outlooks (Folk 2018). Some may simply have been observing "practical

Christianity" and living out Gospel mandates to help and serve the needy. Others were committed to overcoming racism by direct action. Still others wanted to develop a revolutionary cadre to destroy capitalist society. Regardless of the interior motivation, the exterior results were visible and seemed to speak for themselves: the creation of a community in a (failed) attempt to develop a new society that transcended race, class, and gender divisions. We can trace the development of this pluralism through the Temple's different locations – Indiana, California, and Guyana – where civil rights organizing was superseded by progressive politics and anticolonialism was realized concretely in a new nation. The Temple expanded from local politics in Indianapolis, to state and national politics in California, to international affairs in Guyana.

Politics in Indiana

In various autobiographical statements, Jim Jones claimed that he came to communism at an early age (J. Jones 1977; FBI Audiotape Q134 1977). As a child, while World War II raged across Europe, he pretended to kill Nazis at the Battle of Stalingrad. When the war ended, he began to read books about Russia and, by the time he was a senior in high school, he was a communist. He stated that a Communist Party member befriended him and helped keep him out of prison. At Indiana University, he "immediately became an activist, Party organizer" but didn't join the Communist Party of the United States (CPUSA) (J. Jones 1977). Although he eventually found Mao Zedong influential, his first and primary love was Josef Stalin. "I would never accept that Stalin was as bad as he was portrayed," he asserted, though he did acknowledge Stalin's purges of opponents (J. Jones 1977). When the CPUSA broke with Stalin, Jones broke with the CPUSA. "I became my own brand of Marxist," he declared (FBI Audiotape Q134 1977).

This perhaps is the most accurate description of Jones's political outlook – his own brand, one that used Christianity as a front for his Marxism, at least initially. In autobiographical comments, Jones said that he consciously made a decision to infiltrate the church (FBI Audiotape Q134 1977). He did not mention his communist outlook in his early years as a pastor and revivalist, but he did preach for integration and against war, "throwing in some Communist philosophy" along the way (J. Jones 1977). He found Pentecostalists the most accepting of all churches, certainly more accepting of African Americans than mainline denominations. Jones said that he utilized the façade of religion to hide his political views until he deemed it safe to reveal them. In later years, "there wasn't a person that attended any of my meetings that did not hear me say, at some time, that I was a Communist" (FBI Audiotape Q134 1977).

Indianapolis in the 1950s was a good place to put into practice a "Pentecostal Marxism" centered on racial justice. By the end of the fifties, about 15 percent of the population of Indianapolis was African American (Thornbrough 2000: 116). Housing was decidedly inadequate due to neighborhood covenants, real estate practices, and bank resistance. Virtually no homes were available to Blacks for purchase. And when African Americans did buy housing, they precipitated White flight into the suburbs. The Temple's efforts to help its members obtain adequate housing was therefore both political and charitable. A newspaper ad promoting services at the Peoples Temple Full Gospel Church announced that "God has created a perfectly sweet interracial fellowship in all matters in the Temple and outsiders in the neighborhood are rapidly accepting our message. Another all white section broke down. 3 Negro families have moved into our section" ("Peoples Temple Ad" 1955).

The Temple and its pastor achieved a measure of recognition for their integration efforts when the mayor of Indianapolis appointed Jones to direct the Commission on Human Rights in 1961, a position not fully funded until 1958 (Thornbrough 2000: 123). During his brief tenure, Jones and the Temple engaged in subtle persuasion, rather than direct action, to encourage restaurants to serve African Americans and to inspire local businesses to hire Black employees. "By the end of 1961, Indianapolis was a significantly more integrated city than it had been twelve months earlier, and Jim Jones was almost entirely responsible" (Guinn 2017: 104).

Politics in California

While Jones's prediction of nuclear disaster is the usual explanation for the migration to California, and though the desire to emulate Father Divine's back-to-the-land program was another possible motive, a third reason may have been the desire to live out socialist ideals in a more progressive environment. "Beyond simply moving to the center of black political activity in the U.S., the relocation of Peoples Temple … signaled its entrance into a broader coalition of leftist organizations and a new level of visibility" (Harris & Waterman 2004: 106). Whereas the socialism of Pentecostal Christianity resided in the practice of the early church, in which members sold their possessions and shared all things in common (FBI Audiotape Q134 1977), the socialism of California took a decidedly more militant stance.

Temple members heard about socialism directly from the pulpit in Redwood Valley. In one videotaped sermon, Jones stated that he came in the guise of religion to free people from religion. He denigrated the God of heaven and proclaimed that "God is perfect freedom, justice, equality, and thus the only thing that brings perfect justice, freedom, and equality, perfect love in all of its beauty and holiness, is socialism. Socialism is God" (J. Jones 1972?). He distinctly claimed to be God throughout the sermon and explained that, in the current dispensation, "I came as a god, socialism, to eliminate all your false gods." When he announced that socialism is God, the congregation jumped to its feet, amplifying the "amens" and "right ons" with raised fists. "God is a socialist worker," Jones asserted. "He's one of the people."

Good works characterized the public activities of Peoples Temple in Redwood Valley and San Francisco, but behind closed doors, a program of discipline and behavioral conditioning occurred in catharsis sessions. Discipline was administered in the Temple for what society considers bad behavior – lying, stealing, cheating, hitting, and so on (Moore 2011). A child who bit someone was bitten. A person who stole was assigned street-corner begging. Children who shoplifted were spanked (Roller 1975). Behavioral modification differed from discipline in that it targeted social mores rather than illegal or immoral infractions (Moore 2011). The punishment for violating the new, socialist ethos was tailored to the crime. Being ageist could mean helping seniors after school for a week; laziness and irresponsibility might require laboring in menial tasks around church buildings. Some misconduct resulted in corporal punishment. Being sexist might require boxing with a girl. Other transgressions merited spanking, paddling with a board, or receiving a beating.

Members confessed their wrongdoing publicly, within the congregation, or wrote down private responses to questions posed, even if they had to make up their own sins. Everyone was expected to "admit" to having homosexual urges, to molesting their own children, and to desiring sex with Jim Jones. But members also readily conceded ordinary breaches of socialist practice. For example, one young man had to engage in a fight for calling a Black Temple leader an Uncle Tom and calling a White Temple leader a racist (Roller 1976d). With the congregation's approval, three women hit a young man because he was cheating on his girlfriend; they also slapped his new partner for helping the original girlfriend get an abortion. Then the young man and his partner had to kneel and kiss the feet of the original girlfriend (Roller 1976d).

While social conditioning occurred privately within the Temple, public lectures and presentations educated members and outsiders alike about current social issues. A range of political figures made appearances on Temple stages in San Francisco and Los Angeles. These included prominent world figures as well as local dignitaries and officials. Chilean refugees Laura Allende and Orlando Letelier spoke at the Temple about the persecution they endured under the right-wing coup in Chile. Daniel Ellsberg talked about the Pentagon papers. Harvey

Figure 4 Temple members Richard Paar (extreme left), Wesley Johnson, Barbra Hickson, Ricky Johnson, and Sandra Cobb walk a picket line in San Francisco to protest eviction of low-income tenants at the International Hotel, 1977. Photo by Nancy Wong. Courtesy of Wikimedia

Milk, the first openly gay county supervisor in San Francisco, made frequent appearances, as did San Francisco mayor George Moscone, several California state legislators, and Black communist university professor Angela Davis.

Temple members in California not only listened to influential leaders; they also engaged in direct action and coalition politics. They protested the eviction of poor senior citizens from the International Hotel, joined with the Socialist Workers Party to denounce racism in South Africa, and boycotted Florida orange juice to protest Anita Bryant's stance against gay people. "Peoples Temple became one of the progressive churches, like Glide Memorial, that allied with New Left and counterculture politics" (Hall 2004: 161). They also provided modest financial support to a variety of local causes: a senior assistance program, a neighborhood health clinic, an animal protection service, and even a Christmas party for Native American children (Hall 2004).

Temple participation in cooperative ventures was often driven by Jim Jones's publicity goals, however. A frequent speaker at press conferences and rallies for righteous causes – antiracism, anti-apartheid, anti-censorship – Jones was less competent navigating the requirements of coalition politics. Archivist Tanya Hollis conducted a detailed study of the Temple's failure to proactively resist redevelopment of San Francisco's Western Addition

(Hollis 2004). Despite interactions with the city's primary redevelopment agency, and despite Jones's position as chair of the Housing Authority, "Peoples Temple did not address the larger issue of urban renewal with the same energy it devoted to issues such as education and drug rehabilitation" (Hollis 2004: 91). Its lack of interest in joining with other organizations to effect political change was an apparent contradiction with its outspoken political stance. Rather than working within the system to challenge existing bureaucracies, the Temple set up its own alternative bureaucracy for offering a human service ministry to the needy (Hall 2004). Nevertheless, the effective publicity machine of Peoples Temple – managed by a volunteer corps of professional journalists, writers, and street vendors – produced press releases, printed and distributed the biweekly newspaper *Peoples Forum*, and created the impression that the Temple was at the forefront of Black progressive politics in the city.

In many respects it was indeed in the vanguard, if we consider the information it delivered about contemporary issues, especially colonialism, to the Temple's three congregations. Nelson Mandela was still imprisoned in South Africa – Temple members signed and circulated petitions calling for his release. A civil war in Angola between two factions that had achieved independence from Portugal was waged as a Cold War proxy between the United States and the Soviet Union – the Temple took an offering for the people of Angola and Jones announced that $500 would be set aside (Roller 1976b). During a question-and-answer session one Sunday afternoon, members asked about the coup in Portugal that overthrew the right-wing dictatorship, about President Gerald Ford's trip to Helsinki, and whether Russia could be trusted (Roller 1975).

On October 8, 1973, the board of directors of Peoples Temple, meeting in Redwood Valley, took concrete steps to enter the postcolonial world directly by adopting a resolution to establish a "branch church and agricultural mission" in Guyana ("Resolution to Establish Agricultural Mission" 1973). In the early 1960s, Jones scouted Cuba, British Guiana, and Brazil as possible locations for resettlement. Temple scouts reconnoitered other places in the early 1970s – Grenada, Bermuda, Trinidad, Peru, and Kenya. But, according to the resolution, Guyana's proximity to the United States, its English-speaking population, its economy – "typical of so-called underdeveloped nations" – and the government's policy of encouraging agricultural projects were all sound reasons for working with the newly independent nation.

The reasons for choosing Guyana seem evident today. The reasons for leaving the United States, however, are not as immediately clear, but, as Jones explained in a lengthy meeting directly after the board adopted the resolution, he saw two threats on the horizon: nuclear apocalypse and dictatorship. Temple members were ready for the apocalypse but not for dictatorship, so they "have to be prepared to go to *other* places in the world if a dictatorship takes over, because I *told* you … not one of my children's gonna end up in a concentration camp" (FBI Audiotape Q958 1973, italics in original). Jones proposed buying a plane to help people escape the Babylon in which they were living. "I don't want to *leave* this country – this is our country – but I don't intend to stay here if they take it over with a dictatorship." Fears of a dictatorship were not entirely unfounded given revelations of the secret COINTELPRO actions that the FBI conducted against African American leaders, leftist groups, and the Communist Party between 1956 and 1971. Throughout the 1970s, Cold War politics rationalized unconstitutional and illegal behavior by many government bodies and individuals charged with enforcing the law.

In the 1973 exhortation to move, Jones alluded to Marcus Garvey (1887–1940) and the Jamaican leader's quest for freedom abroad. Active in the 1920s, Garvey was the founder of the Universal Negro Improvement Association and a proponent of Blacks moving back to Africa, where they would be welcome. On other occasions, Jones turned to many themes familiar to African Americans: exile and exodus, the Great Migration from the American South to the North, the Babylon that is America, but especially the Promised Land – the term that became shorthand for the agricultural project in Guyana and that summarized the hopes and aspirations of those in the Temple. "To him, the convergence of different oppressed people's plights underscored the need for flight to safe haven" (Hall 2004: 176). By the end of 1973, an advance team made up of key Temple leaders and Jones himself met with government officials in Guyana. Work began on the agricultural project in early 1974.

Politics in Guyana

Guyana had its own reasons for welcoming a group of US expatriates of largely African descent. Less than a decade after independence in 1966, the tiny nation on the north coast of South America faced severe economic problems. Prices for its sugar-related products were down and an embargo on the export of oil imposed by Arab oil-producing states drove prices up (Guinn 2017: 293–4). Infusing millions of dollars into the Guyana economy, Peoples Temple provided more financial aid to the struggling nation than did the US government (Poster 2019). A border conflict with Venezuela to the west also raised concerns. Placing a group of Americans in the disputed area – already being developed as "Venezuelan Guayana" by the Venezuelan government – might well discourage actual military intervention and was "less expensive than buying bombers and bazookas and building air-raid shelters" (Crist 1981: 110–11, original spelling). Moreover, the majority of Guyana's eight hundred and fifty thousand residents lived along the coast or near one of the many rivers. The government of Guyana sponsored its own agricultural projects away from population centers in the hope of relocating some of its citizens. A successful settlement by Americans in the interior might demonstrate to the Guyanese the possibilities inherent in such development, especially to those living near the leasehold. Influenced by its close ties to the Democratic People's Republic of Korea and its philosophy of self-reliance, self-discipline, and self-sacrifice, Guyana's government hoped to retrain and relocate people into agricultural production (Taylor 2015).

There was some irony, however, in Peoples Temple trading a presumed dictatorship in the United States for an actual dictatorship in Guyana. The leaders of the Peoples National Congress (PNC), the ruling party in the 1970s, were indebted to covert intervention by the United States and the United Kingdom to rig the elections that led to independence (Poster 2019). Opposition parties were repressed and political opponents were harassed, beaten, exiled, and – in the case of outspoken Black activist Walter Rodney – assassinated. The difference, it seems, was that the Temple supported the PNC, bestowing party leaders with gifts and pumping money into the Guyana economy in exchange for the privilege of living outside of government oversight. "A free state of Jones" existed in which a "government within a government" ruled (Poster 2019: 319, 322). Temple aides who lived in Georgetown acted more or less as diplomatic envoys between Peoples Temple and foreign governments, meeting regularly with officials, including ambassadors, at the Cuban, North Korean, and Soviet embassies. They also maintained frequent contact with ministers in the Guyana government.

Although the government of Guyana and Peoples Temple reached a tentative agreement to start clearing land in 1974, it was not until February 1976 that the parties signed a formal lease for twenty-five years granting the use of 3,852 acres at the rate of twenty-five cents per acre ("Guyana Land Lease" 1976). When US ambassador Max Krebs visited the settlement in March 1975, he found a six-mile-long swath of roadway leading to the projected center of the agricultural project, 25 acres already under cultivation, and a "relaxed and informal" atmosphere among the pioneers. "My impression was of a highly motivated, mainly self-disciplined group, and of an operation which had a good chance of at least initial success" (Krebs 1978: 135). In May 1976, another embassy staff member observed a dozen tractors and heavy agricultural equipment, 100 acres under cultivation, with more land being cleared, and about six "rustic buildings" (Matthews 1978). Don Beck, one of the pioneers, went to Jonestown in summer 1976 to provide schooling for the ten children living there. With about thirty-five residents total, it was extremely small, "peaceful, beautiful, a place of equality and mutual respect and support" (Beck 2005b).

As the new year began, only forty people lived in what Beck called "almost a paradise." But by December 1977, seven hundred Temple members had crowded into housing intended for a few hundred. The massive influx lowered living conditions: the quality of food, housing, healthcare, and sanitation began a slow decline. Even so, the standard of living for Jonestown residents was no worse than that of their Guyanese neighbors and, in some respects, it was a good deal better. They had a medical clinic, programs for seniors and education for children, a sawmill for producing revenue, and, should they decide to use them, large financial reserves.

Conflict with the US Government and the Media

While it is true that the arrival of Jim Jones in June 1977 marked a turning point, numerous dynamics contributed both to his immigration and to the ever-changing situation in Jonestown. Most important was the formation of the Concerned Relatives in 1977, a group made up of former members and those related to current members of Peoples Temple. "Cultural opponents" like the Concerned Relatives frame new religious movements as imperiling the established order (Hall with Schuyler & Trinh 2000: 12). This then justifies the actions they take. Even before a formal group was established, ex-members contributed to a critical exposé of life in Peoples Temple published in *New West* magazine in 1977 (Kilduff & Tracy 1977). Working with the news media and government agencies, the Concerned Relatives mobilized an effective and successful attack on Peoples Temple. Persuading the Federal Communications Commission to investigate radio contact between Guyana and the United States and alerting the Social Security Administration that Social Security recipients had left the country jeopardized the survival of Jonestown. The Concerned Relatives targeted Jim Jones, but the entire group suffered.

Although members fled the United States in order to find sanctuary abroad, their conflict with the Concerned Relatives became a defining issue in the Promised Land. Indeed, "it [was] no longer possible to understand Peoples Temple apart from the actions of its detractors" (Hall 2004: 289). A custody battle over John Victor Stoen (1972–8), a child Jones claimed to have fathered, created a crisis mentality in the community. If Tim and Grace Stoen succeeded in forcing the child's return to the United States, would other relatives seek custody as well? And how would Jones's pledge to defend all of his followers remain credible? As a result of sustained pressure from an organized opposition, their leader's growing paranoia, and perhaps a level of malnutrition that impaired the decision-makers in Jonestown, conditions deteriorated in 1978.

While discipline and behavioral modification characterized indoctrination methods of the Temple in California, behavior control and terror became the strategy in Jonestown (Moore 2011). Residents of Jonestown not only engaged in self-criticism but also reported on fellow residents. In a small community, everyone knew everyone else's business – who was a slacker, who was stealing food, and who had a bad attitude. The administrators of various departments – agriculture, sewing, medical, construction, and so on – wrote detailed reports on each worker in their department. These reports were then read at Peoples Rallies for praise and punishment. Those doing well, who were hard workers and had a good attitude, were commended; those who were not were assigned to the Learning Crew, in which they performed extra work on top of regularly assigned duties. The Learning Crew did some of the toughest labor, such as digging ditches, cleaning latrines, and weeding crops. Some residents, including children, were "sent out to the tiger," a form of terror in which the disobedient were taken into the jungle in the darkness, tied to a tree, and waited to be eaten. The terror lay in the imagination, not in the reality. For those who remained recalcitrant, a "seldom-used" underground isolation box was created in February 1978, in which sensory deprivation of a few days was intended to change the troublemaker's behavior (Hall 2004: 240–1). The most resistant, or dissident, received heavy sedation in the Special Care Unit, although fewer than a dozen seemed to get this treatment. Thus, Jonestown became "a highly charged zone of crisis" as the Concerned Relatives increased the pressure and were seen as "endangering the life of the community" (Chidester 2003: 143).

Yet the hope remained that residents would become good socialists ready to make a final migration to a welcoming communist country. The Georgetown Temple staff asked representatives of the Yugoslavian, Cuban, and North Korean embassies if they would host the group as immigrants. But the most desired place for immigration was Russia. Everyone in Jonestown practiced speaking the Russian language, and all diligently studied Marxism and postcolonial current events. The news that residents got via Jim Jones came directly from Eastern Bloc news feeds, including Pravda and Tass; in fact, a correspondent for Tass visited Jonestown in April 1978 ("Guestbook" n.d.). A Soviet Embassy official visited Jonestown in October 1978 and left impressed with what he saw. A detailed list of selling points for Temple members to use to influence their Soviet interlocutors included highlighting the advantage Americans had of knowing the capitalist mindset ("Peoples Temple Meetings with the Soviet Embassy" 1978).

A collectivist consciousness was inculcated in all aspects of daily life: work, the meetings called Peoples Rallies, and even entertainment. An inventory of videotapes gathered by the FBI from Jonestown included propaganda films from the Soviet Union, a Richard Pryor comedy special, multiple episodes of *Sesame Street*, political films such as *Parallax View*, *Rollerball*, *The Klansman*, and many more (RYMUR 89-4286-2096 1979). The Jonestown Library contained books by Anne Frank, Leo Huberman, Theodore Roszak, Mark Twain, and Richard Wright, among others. Books by Philip Agee and Victor Marchetti provided accounts of CIA misconduct ("The Books of the Jonestown Library" 2012). Popular songs were given new, revolutionary words and familiar songs were heard in the context of a commitment to socialism (e.g., FBI Audiotape Q432 1978). The Temple was no longer a church but rather an experiment in communalism and a realization of socialist ideals.

Meanwhile, the Concerned Relatives increased pressure on the community. The group issued its Statement of Human Rights Violations in April 1978, charging Jim Jones (but not the Temple) with censoring mail, prohibiting phone calls, and preventing visits with family members (Concerned Relatives 1978). Deborah Layton Blakey, a financial secretary, defected in May and publicly reported suicide rehearsals the next month (D. Blakey 1978). The Concerned Relatives launched a letter-writing campaign to members of Congress and the US Department of State demanding an investigation of Jonestown. Under the guidance of former Temple leaders – particularly Tim Stoen and Al and Jeannie Mills (who changed their names from Elmer and Deanna Mertle after they left the Temple) – family members initiated lawsuits against the Temple to regain property. They flooded the State Department with requests to check up on relatives in Jonestown. Taking a page from the Peoples Temple playbook, the Concerned Relatives successfully captured both media and government attention by writing letters, making personal visits, and holding press conferences. "Jones *was* the object of a network of opposition that included defectors, reporters, and government agencies" (Hall 2004: 215, italics in original).

Jonestown residents were well aware of these efforts and fears of invasion escalated. Security was tightened. Dissidents were harshly punished. Civil defense drills, suicide rehearsals, and other preparations for resistance occurred under the heading White Night, a catch-all term that covered a commitment to fight and a willingness to die (McGehee 2013a). In letters and public statements, residents declared their readiness to die for the Cause. One mother, for example, wrote that she believed in revolutionary suicide and would "take care of" her children if the need arose (J. Carter 1978). Others described the ways in which they would "take care of" enemies. Thus, the Concerned Relatives demonized Jim Jones and residents of Jonestown demonized Tim Stoen and the relatives.

Both groups reacted and responded to each others' provocations in what scholars identify as an interactive process that can lead to violence (e.g., Hall with Schuyler & Trinh 2000; Wessinger 2000; Bromley 2002; Wessinger 2008).

A rhetoric of self-sacrifice defined, in part, the social and political movements of the 1960s and 1970s. Political assassinations, police shootings, and the murders of civil rights activists convinced Black militants that taking a stand against the system was a form of "revolutionary suicide," in the words of Huey P. Newton, a leader of the Black Panther Party (Newton 1973). Death was not the goal, liberation was, but given the machinery of the state, death was a real possibility. While the rhetoric of the time seems bombastic and self-aggrandizing today, it is important to recall that militants in that era sincerely believed they were engaged in a life-and-death struggle (Moore 2013). A well-documented culture of violence against them indicated that their analysis was correct.

When Congressman Leo Ryan announced his intention to visit Jonestown, he not only set in motion the Temple's immediate plans for self-destruction but also confirmed the teachings that members had been hearing for many years – there was a conspiracy against them that would not let them live in peace, no matter where they went. Residents signed a petition dated November 9 protesting Ryan's visit and stating that they had neither invited him nor would welcome him – or reporters or "concerned citizens" – into their community ("Jonestown Petition to Block Rep. Ryan" 1978). The next day, a resolution gave notice that anyone associated with Ryan's party, the Concerned Relatives, or the news media would "not be permitted entry within the boundaries of the said Peoples Temple leasehold" and that the community had sought help from the government of Guyana to protect its properties from trespassers ("Resolution of Peoples Temple to Block Rep. Leo Ryan from Entering Jonestown" 1978). The group then issued a press release, which asserted that Ryan's visit "is being staged for the purpose of manufacturing adverse publicity for the Jonestown community, hopefully by provoking some sort of incident" ("Statement of 13 November 1978" 1978).

Certainly Jonestown residents had cause for alarm given the fact that members of the Concerned Relatives and hostile journalists were coming with Ryan. Family members included Tim and Grace Stoen; Jim Cobb and Wayne Pietila, two of the eight revolutionary defectors in 1973; and others who had filed lawsuits against the Temple. Journalists included Tim Reiterman, who had written critical articles for the *San Francisco Examiner*, and Gordon Lindsay, a freelance reporter for the *National Enquirer* whose critical story and silence were purchased by the Temple for the sum of $10,000 (McGehee 2013b). A team of five reporters from NBC News accompanied the Ryan party, along with other representatives of the media. Finally, there was the power of the US government itself, embodied in Congressman Leo Ryan and his staff.

Had the congressman come a few months earlier or a few months later, he might well have encountered a different situation. The fact that a near-massacre was averted in 1977 – thanks to the intervention of officials in Guyana, Angela Davis in the United States, and Temple members in San Francisco – indicates one alternative outcome. Had he arrived in May, before the defection of Deborah Layton Blakey, the possibility of mass death would have been greatly reduced. Had he arrived in January, it is likely that new leadership in Jonestown would have shelved plans for mass death. But rather than simply stage a press conference at the gates of Jonestown, as he had planned, Leo Ryan and his party entered the community, thereby triggering implementation of a scheme that had been discussed many times and rehearsed about a half dozen times. Although Mary Maaga argues that the defection of core White members who left with Ryan ignited the mass suicides (Maaga 1998: 126–7), it seems more likely that the congressman's visit itself – which presaged the undoing of the entire Jonestown enterprise – was the actual spark.

In fact, Peoples Temple members had publicly telegraphed their intent to die on at least four occasions in 1978: in a letter written to Members of the US Congress in March; in a sworn affidavit made by former member Yolanda D. A. Crawford in April; in a press release from Peoples Temple issued in May; and in an affidavit sworn by another former member, Deborah Layton Blakey, also in May (Moore 2022a). Blakey announced the existence of suicide rehearsals not only to the news media at a press conference but also to officials in the US Department of State and to Congressman Ryan himself. State Department officials reminded Ryan that he had no legal authority in Guyana and warned him several times that he would not be welcome in Jonestown. In other words, the congressman ignored the facts at his disposal when he embarked on his final journey.

The assassination of Congressman Ryan on the Port Kaituma airstrip seems impromptu compared to the careful planning that went into organizing the mass deaths in Jonestown. Apart from the children and those senior citizens found dead in their beds, it is difficult to say how many others were murdered that day. In Georgetown, Temple loyalist Sharon Amos clearly murdered her three children before killing herself, responding to orders given in code from Jonestown through shortwave radio, but others living in the capital city did not follow her example. In Jonestown, certainly some resisted while some were too exhausted to resist. Some saw their children die, and they may have been more willing than most to follow them in death. Some saw this as the sacrificial death they had prepared for their entire Temple lives. The author's sister Annie wrote in 1973 that she wanted to be in on changing the world "to be a better place and I would give my life for it" (Moore 1986: 94). On November 18, 1978, she took her own life.

But one voice of dissent spoke up as the deaths were occurring. Christine Miller asked, "Is it too late for Russia?" Jones responded that it was because of the killings at the airstrip (FBI Audiotape Q042 1978). Miller persisted, suggesting that they use an emergency code for making an airlift to Russia. "I don't think nothing is impossible if you believe it," she declared. But Jones denied that such a code existed, adding, "We can check with Russia to see if they'll take us in immediately, otherwise we die" (FBI Audiotape Q042 1978). Miller's question was not unfounded since many documents indicate that residents of Jonestown sincerely believed they were going to move to the Soviet Union ("Peoples Temple Meetings with the Soviet Embassy" 1978). A few months or weeks before the final day, they even signed a petition expressing their desire to "emigrate to the Soviet Union" ("Petition to Move to the Soviet Union" 1978).

The members of Peoples Temple might have been naïve, unsophisticated, and perhaps uneducated regarding doctrinaire Marxism–Leninism. Nevertheless, they believed they were socialists at the least and exemplary communists at best. For the most part, however, those on the left denied any link between the Temple's socialism and communism and their own. Huey Newton disavowed Jones's understanding of revolutionary suicide (Naipaul 1980: 287–8). Other analysts argued that Jonestown was the product of "non-Marxist varieties of communist thought which were explicitly criticized by Karl Marx and Frederick Engels under such terms as 'utopian socialism' and 'crude communism'" (Mrett 2020). Or they characterized Jim Jones as "an obscure socialist thinker, blending elements of atheism, Christianity, Marxism, Leninism, Maoism, and Third World revolutionary rhetoric into a complicated brew of political sentiments" (Harris & Waterman 2004: 106). In contrast, Marxist blogger Gus Breslauer asserted that, "despite their fate, members of Peoples Temple were communists" (Breslauer 2021). Left-wing groups are no more immune to the cultlike following of charismatic leaders than any others, and they perhaps may be more susceptible given their idealistic challenge to mainstream society.

4 The Economics of Peoples Temple

If the political ideology of socialism was sacralized under the rubric of apostolic socialism, the economics of the faith were lived out in the communalist structure of Peoples Temple. Support for the Temple and its programs began in traditional church fundraising programs: bake sales, raffles, thrift shops, and most especially the weekly offerings, enhanced in Indiana with Jim Jones's collections on the revival circuit. But even in Indiana, new sources of revenue developed in the establishment of nursing homes run by low-paid and volunteer staff who were Temple members. Business ventures continued to develop in California, and more than a half dozen care facilities run by Temple members opened in the Redwood Valley area, sources of housing, employment, and income. The extension of activities to the urban centers of San Francisco and Los Angeles increased the weekly take at worship services far beyond what could be raised in the Valley. In addition, foster care homes for children and life-care contracts for senior citizens brought in county, state, and federal money (in the form of Social Security and disability payments). The turn to communal living also allowed the group to increase revenues by pooling resources for the support and maintenance of its members. Finally, the move to Guyana enabled the complete communalization of those who made their home in Jonestown. No one was paid for their toil, but no one had to buy anything either. All labor was directed toward maintaining the village of a thousand people with the ultimate goal of running a self-sustaining community subsidized by the sale of crops, handmade products, and other services.

And it might have worked. Were it not for the megalomania of Jim Jones, the sycophancy of a leadership cadre, and the relentless pressure of the triad of the Concerned Relatives, the news media, and government agencies, apostolic socialism had a fair chance of success. It began with hundreds of individuals living communally in California and grew into an agricultural project of one thousand. "Apostolic socialism was not a lofty dream," according to John R. Hall. "The communal organization of Peoples Temple became their social world" (Hall 2004: 91). The sociologist of religion went on to point out the tremendous savings due to economies of scale that were poured back into the Temple. With consumption "collectivized" in the sense that the Temple provided the basic necessities for many members, the group was able to amass great wealth.

Sociologist David Feltmate called this the "lost legacy" of Peoples Temple, subsumed in the tragedy of Jonestown. He argued that apostolic socialism was a viable economic program worth investigating. Extrapolating from figures developed in 1988 (Hall 1988), Feltmate found that the nine hundred residents of Jonestown would have received $43,712 per person in 2017 dollars. If the assets were distributed equally, "Temple members … would be wealthier than the majority of their fellow Americans today" (Feltmate 2018: 124).

Indiana

In the first half of the 1950s, Jim Jones worked at several churches in Indianapolis and preached on the revival circuit before founding Peoples

Temple. As an independent church with no denominational affiliation or support, the Temple provided no salary or parsonage. Both Jim and Marceline worked to support themselves and their church. Jim held a number of odd jobs, including importing and selling monkeys for a time (Reiterman with Jacobs 1982: 60). But his biggest earnings continued to come from speaking at revivals throughout the upper Midwest rather than from the offerings of low-wage members of his congregation. A popular speaker, "he could've taken that Oral Roberts trip but he wouldn't do it," according to his wife (M. Jones n.d.[a]). A registered nurse, Marceline took the lead in establishing the Temple's first nursing home in their own household, a step that led to formal incorporation in order to assume the management of additional nursing homes in Indianapolis (Guinn 2017: 82). The homes provided care for the needy, jobs for members, and income for the Temple, letting Jones purchase radio time and allowing members to distribute clothing at no cost and to open a free restaurant. Advertisements in local papers from the period announced that the Temple also served two free meals every Sunday – one at noon and one at 5:00 p.m.

The similarity between Father Divine's Heavenly Banquets and Peoples Temple's free restaurant and Sunday feedings was no accident. Jim and Marceline frequently visited the Peace Mission in Philadelphia, where Jim was visibly influenced by Father Divine. It is notable that an undated set of proposed bylaws for Wings of Deliverance – the precursor to Peoples Temple established by Jim, Marceline, and Jim's mother, Lynetta Jones – mimicked Divine's operation. The document clearly reflected the organization of Peace Mission extensions, or local churches, which operated independently of Father Divine and yet delivered wealth and followers back to him ("Proposed By-Laws for Wings of Deliverance" n.d.). The idea of church extensions briefly existed in the presence of a Peoples Temple branch in Dayton, Ohio.

And, just as Father Divine broadened his scope from the urban center of Harlem into the White rural precincts of Upstate New York, Jim and Marceline moved their integrated congregation from the Black core of Indianapolis to White rural Redwood Valley. Peace Mission members bought property and engaged in agricultural pursuits in what they called the Promised Land (Mabee 2008: 9); Temple members followed the same economic practices in Northern California. Yet there was an important difference between Father Divine and "Daddy Jones" (Lincoln & Mamiya 2004). Divine worked within the capitalist system and encouraged small business development. He did not abolish private ownership, although he did expect individuals to contribute generously to the Peace Mission. In contrast, Peoples Temple recommended communalism and glorified socialism. The group, rather than the individual, was expected to hold ownership for the benefit of all. Nevertheless, Jones had learned well many of the economics lessons that Father Divine taught.

California

With no church building and a small congregation, the leaders and members of Peoples Temple worked in a variety of jobs and professions in Redwood Valley. Some found employment at the local Masonite factory; some, including Jim Jones, taught in the public schools; some were domestics or laborers. New members from the San Francisco Bay Area – many of whom were young, college-educated, White professionals – found positions in the Mendocino County welfare office and other government agencies. Contrary to popular and scholarly opinion, membership in the Temple was not drawn primarily from the poorest segment of society, but rather from the working and middle classes. Members were bricklayers and salespeople, psychologists and cooks, secretaries and mechanics, lawyers and domestics.

Hall's detailed analysis of Temple finances shows how the group was able to mobilize a significant number of resources in a variety of ways in order to redistribute wealth to members (Hall 1988, 2004). In the early years in Redwood Valley, the Temple had few assets other than volunteer labor. At first, members engaged in "petty money-making schemes" that included bake sales, clothing drives, rummage sales, and the operation of a food truck at public events. But they also monetized high-value donations such as jewelry, furniture, vehicles, and real estate. The Temple bought a small strip mall that housed administrative offices upstairs and a laundromat and other businesses downstairs. In 1971, the Temple purchased a number of houses through debt financing and then leased them to licensed individuals to operate as care homes (Hall 2004: 83). Temple members, rather than the Temple itself, ran the facilities and were the ones liable for taxes, but they turned the profits over to the group. By maintaining a central purchasing office, the Temple could provide supplies to the operators at greatly reduced rates, making the homes both competitive and affordable. Under the guidance of Marceline Jones, the Temple opened nine residential care facilities for senior citizens, six homes for foster children, and a forty-acre ranch for the intellectually impaired called Happy Acres (Hall 2004: 82). All were licensed by the state, and all received high marks from state inspectors.

Equally money-saving, or money-earning, was the shift to communal housing, which began in Redwood Valley. Both nuclear and nonnuclear families cohabited in homes owned by individuals or by the Temple. Formal and informal guardianships increased the number of children present, as did licensed foster homes. It is important to note that several studies undertaken both before and after November 18 have exonerated the Temple of any hint of welfare fraud. Of the dozens of foster children cared for by Peoples Temple members over the years, only a single child in active foster care lived and died in Jonestown (McGehee 2019), while a few care homes remained in operation in the United States. The commitment to communalism expanded in San Francisco, where a conservative estimate identifies thirty-two residences there with more than four hundred individuals living in them ("US Addresses for People Emigrating to Guyana" 1977; excluded from that estimate are those who appear to be a single family living at one address, but included are two or more families living at the same address). Many apartment buildings were either owned by the Temple itself or by Temple members. A number of senior citizens living communally signed up for life-care plans similar to those offered by other religious organizations. In exchange for a monthly fee – or the assignment of financial resources – an individual was fed, housed, clothed, and cared for as long as they lived.

Young adults took an analogous step by "going communal" when they turned over all their assets – wages, property, everything – and lived on the beneficence of the Temple. The author's sisters presented two different examples of this. Both lived communally – Annie at the Temple on Geary Boulevard, Carolyn in an apartment on Page Street – although it is likely that Carolyn lived in the Temple as well given the fact that she had a sexual relationship with Jim Jones. Annie worked as a nurse at San Francisco General Hospital and turned her paycheck over to the Temple. Carolyn, however, worked without wages for the Temple as an administrator. Both submitted needs requests to buy personal items. But, unlike others in the Temple, their parents lived across the Bay Bridge and were able to give them money – which they then passed along to the Temple.

Solicitation for funds was ongoing work. Temple members went on the street to ask for donations – to beg from strangers – either voluntarily or as punishment meted out during catharsis. Cookies and pies were sold after services. Prayer cloths, photos of Jones, and holy oil, all available for purchase at the three churches, brought in thousands of dollars a month (Mills 1979: 180). Al and Jeannie Mills, who defected in 1976 and eventually led the Concerned Relatives group, developed a profitable mail order distribution system for the Temple to extend the sales market for specially anointed cufflinks, photographs, lockets, and other charms to protect the individual from harm. Religious radio programs featured Jim Jones and ran ads soliciting both donations and sales at the programs' conclusion. At its height, the mass mailing program was sending out eleven thousand pieces a month and bringing in "well over $300,000 a year from the media ministry" (Hall 1988: 70S–71S). Donations of real estate, either for Temple members to live in or as a contribution to the Temple, were profitable. And of course the regular offering plate was passed around multiple times during each service, with services at three locations. It all added up.

And where did it all go? Certainly part of it financed the human service ministry the Temple boasted of – legal aid for those in landlord-tenant disputes and minor civil actions, free feeding programs, free health services, low-income rental units. Another part maintained facilities in three locations and supported those who subscribed to life care or went communal. A large portion was devoted to the development of the agricultural project in Guyana – $3 million in 1976 alone, with $310,000 allocated to purchase heavy equipment (Hall 2004: 89). Reiterman and Jacobs estimated that the project required a $5 million capital investment (1982: 334). Don Beck's careful analysis of all of the checks written on the three Guyana bank accounts held by the Temple showed where some of the money went in 1977 – from three hundred pairs of boots, to mattresses, to flat steel, to rice, flour, split peas, and tractor parts (Beck 2012).

Even before the mass migration to Guyana in 1977, Jim Jones was searching for ways to hide the group's assets. He was already securing some resources by setting up bank accounts for his wife, his mother, and himself, and was discharging one of the Temple secretaries to buy certificates of deposit in the millions of dollars for the Temple (Guinn 2017: 320–1). Legitimate fears of a tax audit – since the Temple account books were not squeaky clean and unrelated business income was not always reported – were a concern. Chief Temple attorney Tim Stoen researched offshore bank accounts to place the money outside the reach of the US government. When Stoen defected in 1977, the urgency of transferring funds intensified. Top leaders, primarily women, smuggled out cash strapped to their bodies and stashed in their suit-cases to banks in Switzerland, Panama, Guyana, Venezuela, and other Caribbean nations. When the threat of an audit came that same year, the Temple was prepared: San Francisco bank accounts were closed, money was wired to Guyana through Canadian branch banks, and large amounts of cash were brought into Jonestown (Reiterman with Jacobs 1982: 334).

After the deaths occurred and the Temple went into receivership, efforts were made to recover the money. Robert Fabian, the court-appointed receiver, spent several years tracking down millions in foreign bank accounts, safe-deposit boxes, and real estate titles – $13 million was recovered and paid out to relatives, victims of the air-strip shooting, the Justice Department to recoup the cost of the bodylift and the IRS to pay for back taxes, and the receiver himself (Moore 1985: 352, 355).

Guyana

An impending tax audit (Hall 2004), coupled with the threat of bad publicity from an exposé that featured critical accounts of life in the Temple by former members (Kilduff & Tracy 1977), sent Jim Jones and hundreds of Temple members rushing to Jonestown in 1977. Although the article did not come out until August, the mere knowledge of its upcoming publication imperiled the Temple. The group marshaled its supporters in the media and local government, but its pristine image was tarnished. The population of Jonestown jumped from several dozen at the beginning of 1977 to more than seven hundred by the year's end.

Figure 5 Al Simon (lower left) and Paul McCann with chainsaw preparing logs for the sawmill in Jonestown, date unknown. Courtesy of the the Jonestown Institute

How was this extraordinary transfer of people managed? Rhetorical studies scholar Heather Shearer's comprehensive analysis of the emigration documents generated by the move revealed that a combination of "member contributions (labor and money), timing, and – significantly – texts" contributed to this accomplishment (Shearer 2018: 68). She tabulated the variety of texts used to effect this: resolutions, leases, progress reports, planning documents, and immigration forms. Internal documents directed at those contemplating the move included an Application to Go Abroad, a Skills Inventory, a Promised Land Work Preference, a medical release form, and other items. "The data gathered through this application effort was massive" (Shearer 2018: 82). Once a member was approved for emigration, additional documents were provided: packing lists, clothes lists, checklists, and a formal letter of introduction. An enormous amount of labor was required to track all of this paperwork. Indeed, the Temple had established a thoroughly efficient bureaucracy.

The bureaucracy generally worked well in spite of Jim Jones, a micromanager who gave orders rather than delegating decision-making. The hierarchical structure of the organization has been characterized as either a social pyramid (Moore 2018a) or a series of concentric circles (Hall 2004). In both depictions, Jones was the top or central figure, with a layer of close associates carrying out his commands and subsequent layers having less responsibility. At the bottom of the pyramid or on the periphery were the rank and file who knew very little about inner decision-making processes. This explains why survivors have differed in their accounts of life in the Temple and in Jonestown – their social location within the group dictated and shaped their experiences.

The phenomenon of an inner circle of "lieutenants" who carry out the commands of the leader and maintain and enhance the leader's charisma in new religions is well documented (Moore 2021). Scholars call this group charismatic aristocrats, second-order leadership, a spiritual hierarchy, or leadership cadre. These close associates facilitate or deny access to the leader, communicate the leader's wishes and desires, and inflate the leader's status and their own at the same time. White women formed the core of this cadre in Peoples Temple and Jonestown, and their rapid advancement in the administrative ranks of the organization was noteworthy. "There was an opportunity for some women to exercise power and authority beyond what either their gender or educational training would have allowed in mainstream society" (Maaga 1998: 55–6). They managed a million-dollar operation as administrators, secretaries, counselors, lawyers, publicists, financiers, and more. They advanced more rapidly in the bureaucratic ranks than they could have dreamed in the 1970s, a time when the issue of women's liberation was just gaining attention. Their authority often came at the cost of having sex with the leader. Some, like the author's sister Carolyn, were willing to pay the price; others were not. Meanwhile, Black women played an extraordinarily large role in the Temple economy, supplying the womanpower needed for fundraising endeavors. These included running bake sales and clothing drives in the United States, providing Social Security income in Guyana, and performing a range of tasks in Jonestown – from departmental management, to meal planning and cooking, to physical labor.

The White leadership cadre managed Temple affairs in Jonestown and a highly structured bureaucracy replaced the relatively informal PC that once operated in California. More than thirty departments run by eight assistant chief administrative officers (ACAOs) reported to an Administrative Triumvirate (also called the Troika) comprised of Harriet Tropp, Johnny Brown (Jones) and Carolyn Layton (Beck 2013). The ACAOs made up the Steering Committee for the Peoples Rally and Forum, "the primary governing body including all citizens, practicing a total participatory democracy, even of school-age children" ("Jonestown Governmental Responsibility" n.d.). Decisions made by the Steering Committee were subject to review by the executive director – Jim Jones, as listed on organizational charts – and the Peoples Forum. The handful of minutes from Peoples Rallies that are available show that issues of behavior overshadowed issues of community maintenance. More informative were the reports prepared by ACAOs regarding their departments and needs. Notes from a meeting of the agricultural analysts from September 3, 1978, for instance, outlined their needs, problems, and plans. "Wheelbarrows needed said Demosthenes [Kutulas]," the report stated. "Jack [Beam] will get them with Albert [Touchette] and make decision how best to either make them, buy wheels, etc. but will see it gets done" ("September Ag Reports" 1978).

Plenty of secretarial help seemed to be available to type up reports, minutes, test results, and notes from meetings with foreign diplomats. The watchwords in the Temple were "Verbal orders don't go – Write it!" which appeared on a memo pad used during emigration to the Promised Land (Shearer 2018: 73). This accounted for the FBI recovering eleven trunkloads of documents from the community. Sometimes it appears that handwritten items were specially typed so that Jim Jones could read them at his leisure. For example, the answers to questions like "Is Father an atheist?" (yes, but he believes that the mind lives on) or "What is Dad's worst pain?" (the defection of traitors who pretended to love him), demonstrated whether residents were listening to what Jones had to say (RYMUR 89–4286-FF-11-a-50 – 81 1978). Typists also transcribed audiotaped autobiographical reflections given by Jim Jones, Marceline, and Lynetta as well as other community members for later reading and editing.

Many documents demonstrate the extensive management systems required to maintain the community in the jungle: job descriptions, lists of skilled workers, production reports, accounting forms, employee evaluations, and more. Using Temple records the FBI recovered from Jonestown, Beck compiled an inventory of all the jobs in Jonestown, the people who did them, and a reverse inventory of everyone in Jonestown and the jobs they performed (Beck 2013). Labor was more plentiful than it might at first seem. With about 380 children age twenty and under and about 185 seniors sixty-one and over, there appeared to be a nonproductive cohort of more than 560 persons. But teenagers worked in the fields on occasion, school-aged children sometimes served time on the Learning Crew for misbehavior, and seniors were employed making crafts and preparing food. Residents worked in agricultural endeavors, the Jonestown school, health services, public utilities, construction, security, and food and central supply. There was even a department devoted to entertainment and guests.

An analysis by two Guyanese scholars labeled the agricultural project the "Jonestown Plantation" given the preponderance of African Americans working under a White leadership cadre (Matthews & Danns 1980). An analysis of race and job assignments in Jonestown showed that we would expect to see Blacks outnumber Whites in all work categories by a factor of three since 70 percent of the residents of Jonestown were African American (Moore 2017). In the case of laborers in the category of agricultural work crews, 26 out of 121 workers, or about 21 percent, were White, thus tempering the claim that Blacks performed almost all of the manual labor. But that was not true of the leadership roles. The number of White supervisors routinely exceeded that of Black, although some documents indicated parity between the number of White and Black ACAOs. The only departmental category that reflected the actual racial profile of Jonestown was that of Security, which was 70 percent Black. Yet policing boundaries, both geographical and behavioral, was a racially charged task, with Black residents carrying out the role of enforcers. A few members of the security team bore firearms, which increased their authority and enhanced their menace. Despite rumors of an arsenal that circulated before and after the deaths, approximately thirty-two guns and some crossbows were recovered from Jonestown, according to a federal analysis ("Bureau of Alcohol, Tobacco, and Firearms Investigation" 1978).

Regardless of the role or roles residents assumed in the Jonestown bureaucracy, with 70 percent of the population being Black, it is evident that the community could exist neither physically nor financially without Black labor and leadership. Jonestown was cash poor, subsisting chiefly upon the Social Security payments to its senior citizens, which totaled approximately $36,000 per month (McGehee 2002). Moreover, 90 percent of the Social Security recipients were African American. "Seniors are an economic base we need," admitted Carolyn Layton in an analysis of future prospects, "and the youth are a labor force we need" (C. Layton 1978). Sales of crafts made in Jonestown, such as stuffed animals and wooden toys, and street begging in Georgetown provided additional income, as did the offerings contributed back in California. Property transfers that occurred before, during, and after the mass migration also served to raise thousands of dollars. Money should never have been a problem given the fact that millions of dollars were secreted in foreign banks. Even though the Temple was fighting more than a half dozen lawsuits launched by the Concerned Relatives – from efforts to recover donated property to charges of slander to child custody cases – there was still plenty left over to support the agricultural project.

But Jim Jones "had no plans for the future, only the reality of the present, revolutionary moment" (Chidester 2003: 126). Even before Jones became addicted to prescription medication and suffered mental deterioration, multiple audio recordings and documents indicate his fascination with and fixation on death. In a taped sermon from 1972, Jones referred to the possibility of his own suicide: "Some of you are young, you've got lives ahead of you. I face things like having to have the cyanide in the right place" (FBI Audiotape Q955 1972). Diarist Edith Roller reported that at a Saturday night service in 1976, Jones declared that "the last orgasm I'd like to have is death if I could take you all with me" (Roller 1976a). In a similar vein, he announced in Jonestown six months before the deaths that the "only fuck I want right now" is the orgasm of "the fucking grave" (FBI Audiotape Q636 1978). Jones inculcated his obsession in members at the San Francisco Temple through the presentation of documentaries, news accounts, and lectures about torture, repression, and murder. In Jonestown, the preoccupation focused on conspiracies – real and imagined – against the community. Thus, the sustainability of Jonestown was of little consequence to its leader. Indeed, religion scholar James R. Lewis argued that because Jones's health was failing, he may well have decided to take his followers with him on his own suicidal journey, seeing no future for their lives without him (J. Lewis 2005). Forensic literature has identified the familicide-suicide that involves "a depressed father who kills his entire family and then himself, often viewing his act as a delivery of his family from continued hardships or suffering" (Knoll 2008). "Father kills family, self" – the headline that summarizes familicide-suicide – was another possible interpretation of Jones's ultimate motivations.

Furthermore, the leadership cadre, along with rank and file members, were well aware that some of their activities in Jonestown constituted kidnapping, sexual abuse, torture, and other criminal acts. That would explain the reluctance of Jones and others to let people return to the United States, although it would not necessarily prompt them to implement a suicide plan. The party to a bitter custody suit, Jones himself feared arrest if he went to Georgetown for medical treatment. In effect, he had placed himself under house arrest in Jonestown. There was no way out.

Despite Jim Jones and his pathologies, many of which were appropriated by his followers, there is much to be learned from the experiment in apostolic socialism. Despite the racism implicit in the leadership cadre and in the organization of the group, "ultimately, the Temple was able to inspire white and black people to live together in close proximity, a major accomplishment in the United States where … residential patterns remain segregated" (Feltmate 2018: 132). Living and working collectively, Temple members tried to unlearn the habits of a lifetime and develop a new consciousness in order to realize shared goals. Even though the reality of social equality in the Temple did not match its rhetoric, the movement did reveal the possibilities available to religious groups committed to radical change. Using the benefits of tax exemptions, volunteer labor, and bureaucratization – buttressed by ideological commitment – institutions like Peoples Temple promised an eventual convergence of reality with rhetoric, at least within the boundaries of their own structures.

A racially integrated group of dedicated communalists might well have succeeded even or especially in the absence of Jones. The fields were cleared, the equipment was ready, the infrastructure was established, and some funding was available. The Jonestown pioneers worked for three years without Jones's supervision before their leader made Guyana his permanent home. They shared a commitment to the creation of a new society, rather than to a person. It seems entirely possible that they could have continued in the absence of a figurehead. If Jones had died as a result of his drug abuse or chronic illness, or if a coalition of leaders, which might have included his biological son, Stephan, and his wife, Marceline, deposed him, a community of those willing to continue might well have survived.

5 The Afterlives of Peoples Temple

The life and death of Peoples Temple raises existential questions about the nature of human beings and the ways that religious, political, and economic factors shape the decisions people make. David Feltmate argues that new religions attempt to answer the question: "How then should we live?" He observes that they provide many different ways to answer that question by showing us how others have lived and how we might choose to live. "Sometimes they are failed experiments, but that does not mean we should dismiss them" (Feltmate 2016: 95).

The wide range of responses to Peoples Temple, and most especially Jonestown, indicates the polyvalent nature of the group. The contested character of the movement – idealistic, evil, misguided, punitive, utopian – opens up the possibility of multiple readings. Of course, the sex and violence that occurred within the Temple naturally lend themselves to salacious treatments in books, movies, and other popular outlets. But there are also filmmakers, writers, artists, and musicians who have approached the subject with respect for those whose meaning came from their lives and not only their deaths.

Most Jonestown interpreters start from their own beliefs and conclusions and work backward from there. Even a few scholars adopt this approach. Nowhere is this point of departure more evident than in the alternative theories that attempt to explain why "Jonestown" – as a violent event – occurred. There are several reasons for this. Many facts remain in dispute even today concerning not only the deaths in Jonestown but also the quality of life in Peoples Temple during its twenty-five-year existence. Furthermore, the highly stigmatized nature of the deaths, coupled with conflicting news reports at the outset, generated many legitimate questions about what exactly happened. As a result, an enormous body of conspiracy theories has emerged that obfuscates the nature of the movement, sensationalizes the deaths, and continues to exert influence today. Within weeks of the tragedy, conspiracy theories surfaced: a neutron bomb was exploded; the victims were killed by poison gas; heroin was smuggled into the United States in the metal coffins of the dead. In the months and years following the deaths, these theories developed into multiple confabulations that pointed left, right, and center. It was a political hit on a progressive member of Congress. It was a CIA mind control experiment. It was a plot to destroy Black political leadership in San Francisco. Or the conspiracy to perpetrate mass murder and suicide existed, but it was planned by the leadership cadre of Jonestown itself, not by outsiders (Moore 2018e).

Given the political assassinations and culture of violence in American society out of which the Temple arose, the turn to conspiracy theories to explain the deaths was not entirely unfounded. Moreover, Jim Jones and the residents of Jonestown were convinced that a conspiracy against them existed. In that regard they were not mistaken since the Concerned Relatives did act in an organized fashion to not only bring home their family members but also to destroy Jim Jones and Peoples Temple in the process (Lane 1980: 140–1). The degree to which Congressman Ryan's delegation shielded a clandestine goal of dismantling Jonestown is unknown (Hall 2004: 289). The Concerned Relatives prompted investigations by federal and local agencies that indeed threatened the survival of Jonestown. But this is not the kind of documented scheme to interest the conspiracy-minded.

Figure 6 Joyce Touchette holding Gabriella George in Jonestown, 1978. Photo by Doxsee Phares. Courtesy of the Jonestown Institute

The starting point – which is to say, the conclusion from which conspiracy theorists begin – is that people do not voluntarily commit suicide and, more important, parents do not murder their children. Therefore a secret plot must exist to kill them. As sociologist Michael Barkun observes, "A conspiracist worldview implies a universe governed by design rather than by randomness" (Barkun 2013: 3). The plethora of theories that materialized in the immediate aftermath of the tragedy eventually boiled down to the assertion that the CIA was behind the deaths (Judge 1985; Hougan 2003; Whittle 2018a and 2018b). Despite articles debunking this and other unproven claims (Moore 2002; Farrell 2018; Moore 2018f; McGehee 2021a), pseudo-scholarly theories continue to circulate on many websites, recycling demonstrably false information from the same foundational sources.

Like their (dark) mirror counterparts in conspiracy culture, traditional academic scholars continue to consider and reconsider Peoples Temple and Jonestown. Their starting point, however, is the desire to predict and prevent religious violence. A wave of scholarly analyses of Peoples Temple and Jonestown came out in the 1980s (Robbins 1989), but few comparative studies emerged until after the violent encounter between the Branch Davidians and US government agents in 1993. Using the example of Jonestown and other instances of mass murder and suicide, scholars turned to the question of what propels new religious movements toward violence and then answered it in various ways (e.g., Robbins & Anthony 1995; Hall with Schuyler & Trinh

2000; Wessinger 2000; J. Lewis 2005; Wessinger 2008; Moore 2018d). An interactionist theory, which credits both internal and external factors for the descent into violence, became widely accepted. Features within the group, such as the health of the leader(s) and/or its isolation, compete for attention with features outside the group, such as pressure from oppositional groups, government agencies, and the news media. New religions frequently exist in tension with the wider society, and as the conflict between opposing actors heightens, the potential for a final reckoning or "dramatic denouement" escalates (Bromley 2002). The Jonestown tragedy has therefore served as an important benchmark for scholarly assessments of violence and new religions (Melton & Bromley 2009).

In contrast, the starting point for understanding Jonestown for the cult awareness movement (CAM) is the conviction that cults by definition carry the seeds of destruction within them. Those in the CAM see all new religions as inherently dangerous, inevitably beginning their discussions of them with Jonestown as the starting point (Moore 2018c). We see this penchant in the first pages of many anticult works (e.g., Enroth 1979: 13, 15–16; Appel 1983: 1; Singer 2003: 1; Hassan 2019: xviii, 9). Jonestown was a boon to cult experts and deprogrammers – especially at the end of the 1970s, their period of greatest activity until the twenty-first century – because it appeared to ratify their warnings about the danger of cults.

The execution-style murders in February 1980 of Al and Jeannie Mills, the founders of the Concerned Relatives in 1977, and one of their daughters seemed to confirm the existence of a Temple hit squad. (Although law enforcement attention quickly turned to their son Eddie, who was in the house when the murders occurred, no charges were ever filed. Even when the case against Eddie was reopened in 2003, it was swiftly dropped.) The Mills were outspoken critics who met with other defectors on an ad hoc basis for a time before they launched the Concerned Relatives. Like their counterparts in the Temple – and following their own experience when they were members – the Mills taped telephone conversations and shortwave radio communications between Concerned Relatives and family members, and between Temple members and each other. Almost sixty of these tapes ended up with Margaret Singer (1921–2003). The well-known cult expert undoubtedly encouraged the Mills to open the Human Freedom Center (HFC) in 1978 to help others leaving the Temple. The HFC in Berkeley became a hub of activity with bereaved relatives, former members, and survivors of the tragedy gathering to share stories and get help.

The murder of the Mills family was preceded by another post-Jonestown death, the suicide of Mike Prokes in March 1979. Ordered to carry out suitcases full of cash to the Soviet Embassy, Prokes and two other young men left

Jonestown as the deaths were happening. The former newsman, who served as the public relations director for the Temple, called a press conference in his hometown of Modesto, California. He read a statement to the eight reporters assembled in a motel room before entering the bathroom, shutting the door, and fatally shooting himself. In the weeks before his death, he distributed the statement to friends he personally visited. In it, Prokes affirmed what Peoples Temple tried to do in the Jonestown community. The statement also claimed that a government conspiracy brought down Jonestown. A suicide note found with Prokes's body also suggested this. His death was not the result of despondency or a disturbed mind, the note said, but rather a rational act committed for just reasons. "If my death does not prompt another look at what brought about the end of Jonestown, then life wasn't worth living anyway" (Prokes 1979).

Additional suicides and murders followed in the wake of the catastrophe in Guyana. Paula Adams worked in Georgetown as a Temple emissary to the government of Guyana. She became involved with Guyana's ambassador to the United States, Laurence Mann. After the deaths in Jonestown, she moved with Mann to the United States, where they married and she bore their child. They had a bitter separation, however, and in 1983, Mann fatally shot Adams and their son before killing himself. Richard Cordell, who lost twenty-two family members in Jonestown, including his wife and four children, took his own life in 1983. Tyrone Mitchell, whose parents and four of five siblings died, achieved notoriety when he opened fire on a schoolyard, killing one and wounding ten, before he killed himself in 1984. At least one additional murder and suicide occurred in the decades that followed. The number of other social breakdowns – addiction, alcoholism, clinical depression, and so on – is incalculable. It is surprising, then, that there was not more violence, considering the traumatic deaths survivors and relatives encountered.

Survivors Change the Narrative

A week after the deaths in Jonestown, in an unrelated incident, Dan White, a mentally ill former government official, assassinated San Francisco mayor George Moscone and San Francisco County supervisor Harvey Milk. The twin disasters of Jonestown and these assassinations prompted the newly appointed mayor, Dianne Feinstein, to create a task force to protect Temple survivors from violence directed against them, to mobilize resources to help them reintegrate into society, and to provide mental health counseling (Hatcher 1989: 134). Chris Hatcher, a professor of clinical psychology at the University of California, San Francisco, who headed the task force, said that Temple survivors "wanted a chance at a job, any job," and that their primary goal was "to establish stability in their day-to-day lives" (Hatcher 1989: 135). This was easier said than done since some employers refused to assist Temple survivors and, upon learning of an employee's connection to Jonestown, fired them. Moreover, "no Temple members, and almost no relatives came to the mental health centers" established by the city, mainly because some counselors could not deal with those Temple members who confessed to engaging in brutal punishments. Survivors "did not want to try to explain all about the Temple to a naïve professional, however well trained" (Hatcher 1989: 139). Therefore, it is astonishing that survivors had a low rate of subsequent criminal involvement or psychiatric hospitalization. Perhaps not as surprising, many no longer participated in organized religion.

In the years immediately following the deaths, a few survivors attended an annual memorial service held at Evergreen Cemetery in Oakland, California, where the bodies of more than four hundred children and unidentified persons were buried. It wasn't until 2003, however, that survivors – both loyalists and critics – gathered together at the Bay Area home of a former member. The creation of the Alternative Considerations website in 1998 paved the way for this assembly, in part by providing an online venue for news and information exchange and for survivors to publish reflections on their experiences in the Temple. Initial accounts and analyses of what happened in Jonestown that appeared in news stories tended to come from a handful of White apostates and focused on all that was clearly dysfunctional in Peoples Temple. With the passage of twenty years, however, fresh voices began to tell another story. By presenting personal experiences in their own voices, survivors illuminated the reasons people joined the Temple and humanized those who died in Jonestown. Their recollections in turn inspired an extraordinary range of artistic works that took as their starting point the humanity rather than the insanity of Temple members.

Contributing to the reconnection of former Temple members with each other was the development of a play called *The People's Temple* by writers from the Tectonic Theater Project. (The authors inserted an apostrophe in "People's" to differentiate the drama from the group itself.) Best known for *The Laramie Project*, which documented events surrounding the torture and death of Matthew Shepard in 1998, the writers of *The People's Temple* used contemporary personal interviews, audiotapes made in Jonestown, and archival documents to expand popular perceptions of the movement. The play premiered in Berkeley in 2005 with a large group of former members in attendance.

A new narrative began to appear at a meeting of a few survivors and others in early 2001 held at the Z Space, a theater project in San Francisco committed to developing experimental and innovative theater. This marked the first time several members had seen each other since 1978, and it was at times a tearful reunion. Over the course of the next four years, the playwrights pored over the wealth of documents held at the California Historical Society, listened to audiotapes published on the Alternative Considerations website, and interviewed multiple survivors. On several occasions, audiences comprised of survivors viewed staged readings and provided feedback to the writers. Throughout the development process, survivors came together to discuss the play and their experiences among themselves. When the production finally opened, they were able to see what one survivor called "the spirit of PT," presenting the whole picture, both "the dream and the horrific ending" (Kohl 2005).

Interpreting Peoples Temple and Jonestown

Like the playwrights for *The People's Temple*, the Bit Theater group in Babol, Iran, used sources such as sermons, articles, interviews, and memoirs in its "documentary drama" titled *1978*. Although it ostensibly followed the life of Jim Jones and the members of Peoples Temple, the play also included "events, characters, nonlinear time, [and] uncertain location" to create a landscape where "time breaks; the places get lost; and sentences and words turn into voices and sounds" (Shojael 2017). Playwright and director Mohammad Shojael asked: Are there any stories "behind the geometric *mise-en-scène* of the cast or their group singing? Is the audience at the time of Jim Jones' growing influence, looking for an omen and a reference to the environment and the period in which the individual lives?" (Shojael 2017). These questions were directed to Iranian theatergoers who read into the play the experiences of the Iranian Revolution of that same year. Indeed, the playwright intended for audiences to link the revolution and Jonestown as simultaneous events. Produced under conditions of censorship, *1978* served "as a one-word key and watchword for intelligent audiences to flip through their historical memory and will remind them of other temples that were turned into mass graves" (Shojael 2016). In this way, Jonestown worked as a metaphor and a veil for the dashed hopes raised by the Iranian Revolution.

In similar fashion, writers from Guyana utilized Jonestown as figure and allegory to critique colonialism. Wilson Harris's novel *Jonestown* clearly alluded to both the precolonial past of the indigenous people of Guyana and the postcolonial oppression in which the immigrant population lives (Harris 1996). Harris was concerned with memory and history, especially the erasure of the history of precolonial peoples and times. Fred d'Aguiar also addressed colonialism in his volume of poetry about Jonestown, titled *Bill of Rights* (d'Aguiar 1998). He put the event and the place in the larger context of global oppression and domination while at the same time linking Jonestown inextricably to Guyana. Writer and educator Jan Carew looked at Jonestown from the perspective of those native to the Guyanas. In the essay "Jonestown Revisited," Carew's great-uncle Kalinyas, a Carib Indian, takes him to the ruins of the jungle village and commands: "You must write our truth." Kalinyas then relates the history of the area – the indigenous people, the Spanish, the Dutch, the British – before describing his walk among the dead. "They wrote so many words about Jonestown," he says, "but they wrote about themselves. For them, we were invisible" (Carew 2014).

Jonestown continues to loom large in the consciousness of those living in Guyana. When the tragedy struck in 1978, few even knew that a community of Americans lived in the Northwest District. A three-day news embargo by the Guyana government only heightened the mystery. Guyanese who lived as Jonestown neighbors had strange stories to tell, and some accounts entered the realm of folklore (Kohl 2017). For example, a legend concerning the discovery of a suitcase full of money from Jonestown continued to circulate. True or not, the rumor started early on (Reston 1981). Jonestown survivors who returned to Guyana in 2018 met with residents both in the capital city and in the Port Kaituma area near the Jonestown site. While they found that the jungle had obliterated the 3,852-acre project, they also discovered that the Guyanese were eager to share their thoughts and memories.

On the North American continent, African American poets carried Jonestown into different directions. Some of course moved into a critique of the structural racism that prevails in the United States (Parker 1985; Clifton 2012). Audre Lorde's reference to drinking "poisoned grape juice in Jonestown" was part of a larger project in the poem "The Art of Response" in which the poet described how African Americans have responded to the oppression they have endured (Lorde 2000). Still other poets restored humanity to those who died in Jonestown. Carmen Gillespie's book *Jonestown: A Vexation* considers the various ways in which events and personalities are vexing – that is (according to one of the six dictionary definitions she uses), unfixed and unsettled. Her poems capture both the appeal and the terror of Jim Jones and also the beauty of the jungle, the laughter among the people, the magic of the colors (Gillespie 2011). They are designed to vex or muddle all of our preconceptions. A final poet to highlight is darlene anita scott (deliberately all lowercase), whose remarkable poems bring the dead vividly to life (scott 2022). "What I find myself working against (besides the challenges that life presents) is the language that too often surrounds Jonestown: ill-fated, tragic," writes the poet. "The poems that come clearly want to be more than that" (scott 2010).

And so they are, as they reveal the extraordinary in the ordinary life of those who joined the Temple and eventually moved to Guyana.

While Jonestown may lend itself to thoughtful and provocative considerations of life and death in poetry, its ending was red meat for sensationalistic movies and action novels. Most fiction showed little knowledge of Peoples Temple and tended to focus on Jim Jones (Farrell 2012). All dramatic recreations on film thus far made Jones the center of the story. Even the most impartial documentary, Stanley Nelson's *Jonestown: The Life and Death of Peoples Temple*, kept the spotlight on Jones (Nelson 2006). This is why two novels that focused on women in Peoples Temple are so unusual.

Sikivu Hutchinson's *White Nights, Black Paradise* adopted the provocative position that Black women inside and outside the Temple had agency and power to make decisions about their lives (Hutchinson 2015). Hutchinson's first novel incorporated historical figures (Jim Jones), renamed individuals (Marceline Jones is Mablean in the book), composite characters (the African American sisters Hy and Taryn Strayer), and made-up personalities (Ida Lassiter, the Black journalist). The book makes clear what might draw African Americans to the Temple as well as what repels them or makes them skeptical. But, as the title suggests, the Temple and the utopian experiment in Guyana were not pure evil for African Americans. Hutchinson allowed for ambivalence members may have felt and demonstrated the ambiguity inherent in what was essentially a Black movement led by a small corps of Whites.

Beautiful Revolutionary, by Australian novelist Laura Woollett, was a fictionalized account of the life and death of the author's sister Carolyn Layton (Woollett 2018). It was meticulously researched – Woollett spent two months in the United States interviewing people who knew Carolyn and visiting places where she and other members of the Temple lived and worked. Although there were factual elements in the book – for example, Carolyn did indeed bear a son by Jim Jones – most of the story was imaginatively developed. In this instance, as in Hutchinson's book, fiction presented a more accurate picture of Peoples Temple than many fact-based accounts because the authors commenced their projects in the conviction that their characters were not unhappy losers or brainwashed idiots. Rather they were agents of their own destinies who made good and bad decisions for good and bad reasons. Neither author uses Jonestown as the setting for a morality play.

In many respects, artistic representations and music share the same interpretive freedom as fiction and poetry, leaving much to the imagination for viewers and listeners to fill in. There are many pop illustrations of smiling Kool-Aid pitchers, menacing Jim Jones figures, and fields of corpses. These images tell the traditional story of Peoples Temple at a glance. Fine artists, however, complicate the subject matter in pastoral depictions of Jonestown (Gordon 2012) and paintings of storybook animals enacting the Jonestown drama (Brandou 2007). Laura Baird, a Canadian conceptual artist, spent ten years creating the "Jonestown Carpet," a nine-by-twelve foot tapestry based upon David Hume Kennerly's iconic colorful aerial tableau of the Jonestown bodies (Baird 2004). Baird saw her task as trying to discover something that had been lost in all of the aerial photography – and so she did, when one day she saw abstract blotches of color become a banana leaf, a human limb, bodies entwined. Yet the tapestry remains unfinished with a small corner lacking any needlework, "essentially, a blank space" (Baird 2004).

If Baird left a "blank space" for contemplation in her carpet, many musicians have filled the void to overflowing with mash-ups and samplings of audiotapes made throughout the life of Peoples Temple. Most use the words of Jim Jones to present a message relevant to contemporary listeners. For example, Russian musician Sergey Tretyakov sampled Jones's declaration "you're not free" in a way that attacks American consumerism (Tretyakov 2015). The British rock band Alabama 3, known for its radical politics, used Jones's declaration that change must come through the barrel of a gun in its hard-driving song "Mao Tse Tung Said." The group wove samples of Jones's exhortations about the leader of the Chinese Revolution with its own music and political outlook. "The song de-stigmatises Jones' message and dares us to appreciate both the content and the skilful rhetoric. This is genuinely subversive" (Isaacson 2015, original spelling). "Lost Temple," a ten-track album by Dominique Cyprès, adopted a different approach, sampling various tapes made in Jonestown to a musical background, but remaining faithful to the original message. For example, "Pentecostal Socialism" took a sermon by Jim Jones and highlighted his critique of American society, a message still relevant today (Cyprès 2021).

Other musical approaches reflect upon the lives lost and contemplate questions of meaning. Frank Zappa's symphonic piece "Jonestown" (1984) is eerie and meditative. Two ballads – Sofia Talvik's "Jonestown" and Ken Risling's "Down to Jonestown" – raise questions about the purpose of the Jonestown community and the problem of uncritical idealism.

A unique and perhaps the most controversial musical interpretation was the song "Go Outside" by the duo Cults ("Cult Song Includes Temple Images" 2011). The 2011 music video began and ended with news reports from 1978 and seamlessly incorporated the two singers, Brian Oblivion and Madelin Follin, into archival footage of Temple members shot in California and in Jonestown. Sometimes it appears that Temple members are singing to the duo's music; sometimes, the singers lip sync actual dialogue of members.

Figure 7 Plaques installed in 2011 and refurbished in 2018 for the fortieth anniversary of the Jonestown deaths. Courtesy of the Jonestown Institute.

At one point Oblivion is seen leading the children's choir, which prompted Don Beck – the actual choir leader whose image is replaced by Oblivion – to post a complaint to the website on which the song appeared. To Beck's surprise, Isaiah Seret, the director of the award-winning video, responded to his concerns by stating that he wanted to use the footage when he learned that "these were good people, and honestly they were like the people I held close to me, smart, with spiritual inclinations, tolerant, joyful, appreciating their experiences in a shared community" (Beck 2011). Scenes of people laughing and working followed by footage of Leo Ryan's visit to Jonestown and the final day all appear against the background of a bouncy glockenspiel and a catchy tune. By putting the singers directly into Peoples Temple, at least virtually, the video effectively humanized those who died. The images in "Go Outside" offered a dramatic challenge to and a different narrative from the familiar photographs of corpses facedown in the mud.

The Stories Continue

Peoples Temple surely lives on in the expression "drinking the Kool-Aid." The saying has come to signify mindless support, whether of a sports team, a product, or a political personality. Like other slogans that originate in violence – rule of thumb, tit for tat, baker's dozen – its ancestry has been forgotten and "any attempts to eradicate it from the English language would be a quixotic venture" (McGehee 2021b). Yet a modest shift occurred in the twenty-first century, as McGehee noted – news reports of those using the phrase frequently frame it in the history of Jonestown.

The Temple also seems to live on in the memorialization of those who died in Jonestown. In 1979, more than four hundred unidentified and unclaimed bodies were buried in a mass grave in Evergreen Cemetery in Oakland, California. A simple marker noted the spot until 2011, when four large markers listing all who died were set into the ground. The fact that the name of Jim Jones, along with nine hundred and seventeen others, appeared on the plaques became an issue of controversy for some who felt that his inclusion disrespected those whom he led to their deaths. Others saw the monument as simply denoting an important and little-understood event in world history. Thousands of visitors from around the world pay their respects at the gravesite each year.

This pilgrimage seems rather unusual since almost two generations of people have been born who have little if any historical knowledge of the meaning of Kool-Aid or memory of 1978. Individuals under the age of forty come to the subject with a different outlook from their parents. Many are interested in the communal movements and social protests that arose in the twentieth century. Some are fascinated by cults. Both curious and critical, they are open to examining the past for what it has to say about the present. At the same time, their reliance on the Internet for news and information and their captivation by conspiracy theories can make some Millennial and Generation Z researchers credulous and even gullible, believing anything they find that confirms their prejudices. Yet teenagers engaged in National History Day projects, college students writing papers, and graduate researchers developing theses and dissertations demonstrate a high level of sophistication and knowledge when they make inquiries to the Jonestown Institute. Their interests and approaches are vastly different from those adopted in the twentieth century, when discourse concerning the danger of cults dominated discussions of new religious movements. Only with the passage of time could the perspective change, resulting in diverse interpretations of Peoples Temple and Jonestown in the twenty-first century.

The panoply of representations of the events of November 18, 1978, demonstrates the ongoing fascination we have with religion and violence. As one survivor observed, "No one wants to be in a car wreck, but we all stop to look." Until this century, little interest was paid to the actual organization known as Peoples Temple and the people who were part of it. Even now the spotlight remains focused on its leader, Jim Jones. Despite the continuous recycling of forty-year-old accounts that distance us from the people, however, a new generation of scholars, artists, writers, and others is providing fresh insights into what once seemed clear-cut and settled.

"What then is the last word on Jonestown?" asked historian of the Caribbean Gordon Lewis. "It possesses a universal dimension because it speaks to every school of thought, every belief system, in the world in which we live. No one single school can teach self-righteous lessons about it, for the simple reason that it challenges every school to re-examine its central assumptions" (G. Lewis 1979: 47). The story of Peoples Temple and Jonestown is still being written and will continue to be written as long as the human condition remains an ultimate mystery.

Bibliography

Primary Sources

Primary sources include documents, audiotapes, letters, news articles, and other materials generated by Peoples Temple before the deaths in Jonestown and by US government investigators after the deaths. The FBI investigation into the assassination was code-named RYMUR, and some items released under the Freedom of Information Act appear with that designation.

Alternative Considerations of Jonestown and Peoples Temple, hereafter Alternative Considerations. Special Collections and University Archives. San Diego State University. https://jonestown.sdsu.edu

Blakey, D. L. (1978). "Statement of Deborah Layton Blakey." May. Alternative Considerations. https://jonestown.sdsu.edu/?page_id=109651

"Bureau of Alcohol, Tobacco, and Firearms Investigation." (1978). Alternative Considerations. https://jonestown.sdsu.edu/?page_id=13688

Carter, J. (1978). RYMUR 89–4286-EE1-C-34a-b. "Letter to Dad." Alternative Considerations, RYMUR. https://jonestown.sdsu.edu/wp-content/uploads/2013/10/EE1-A-F.pdf

Concerned Relatives. (1978). "Accusation of Human Rights Violations by Rev. James Warren Jones against Our Children and Relatives at the Peoples Temple Jungle Encampment in Guyana, South America." April. Alternative Considerations. https://jonestown.sdsu.edu/?page_id=13081

"The Eight Revolutionaries." (1973). Alternative Considerations. https://jonestown.sdsu.edu/?page_id=14075

FBI Audiotape Q042. (1978). Alternative Considerations. https://jonestown.sdsu.edu/?page_id=29084

FBI Audiotape Q134. (1977). Alternative Considerations. https://jonestown.sdsu.edu/?page_id=27339

FBI Audiotape Q432. (1978). Alternative Considerations. https://jonestown.sdsu.edu/?page_id=27459

FBI Audiotape Q612. (1974). Alternative Considerations. https://jonestown.sdsu.edu/?page_id=27492

FBI Audiotape Q616. (1978). Alternative Considerations. https://jonestown.sdsu.edu/?page_id=66802

FBI Audiotape Q636. (1978). Alternative Considerations. https://jonestown.sdsu.edu/?page_id=27508

FBI Audiotape Q775. (1973). Alternative Considerations. https://jonestown
    .sdsu.edu/?page_id=27582

FBI Audiotape Q887. (1978). Alternative Considerations. https://jonestown
    .sdsu.edu/?page_id=27607

FBI Audiotape Q932. (1972). Alternative Considerations. https://jonestown
    .sdsu.edu/?page_id=27618

FBI Audiotape Q945. (1977). Alternative Considerations. https://jonestown
    .sdsu.edu/?page_id=85637

FBI Audiotape Q955. (1972). Alternative Considerations. https://jonestown
    .sdsu.edu/?page_id=27626

FBI Audiotape Q958. (1973). Alternative Considerations. https://jonestown
    .sdsu.edu/?page_id=60665

FBI Audiotape Q974. (1973). Alternative Considerations. https://jonestown
    .sdsu.edu/?page_id=27630

FBI Audiotape Q1019. (1973). Alternative Considerations. https://jonestown
    .sdsu.edu/?page_id=27305

FBI Audiotape Q1021. (1972). Alternative Considerations. https://jonestown
    .sdsu.edu/?page_id=27307

FBI Audiotape Q1022. (1973). Alternative Considerations. https://jonestown
    .sdsu.edu/?page_id=27308

FBI Audiotape Q1024. (1974). Alternative Considerations. https://jonestown
    .sdsu.edu/?page_id=27310

FBI Audiotape Q1035. (1972). Alternative Considerations. https://jonestown
    .sdsu.edu/?page_id=27316

FBI Audiotape Q1055-1. (1975). Alternative Considerations. https://jonestown
    .sdsu.edu/?page_id=27321

FBI Audiotape Q1055-2. (1966). Alternative Considerations. https://jonestown
    .sdsu.edu/?page_id=27322

FBI Audiotape Q1059-2. (1972). Alternative Considerations. https://jonestown
    .sdsu.edu/?page_id=27332

FBI Audiotape Q1059-3. (1973). Alternative Considerations. https://jonestown
    .sdsu.edu/?page_id=27333

FBI RYMUR. (1978). RYMUR 89–4286-FF-11-a-50–81. Alternative
    Considerations. https://jonestown.sdsu.edu/wp-content/uploads/2013/10/
    FF-9-13.pdf

FBI RYMUR. (1979). RYMUR 89-4286-2096. Alternative Considerations.
    https://jonestown.sdsu.edu/?page_id=87946

"Guestbook." (n.d.). RYMUR 89–4286-C-6. Alternative Considerations.
    https://jonestown.sdsu.edu/wp-content/uploads/2013/10/C-6.pdf

"Guyana Land Lease." (1976). RYMUR 89–4286-A-31-a-21a–A-31–1-21 c. February 25. Alternative Considerations. https://jonestown.sdsu.edu/?page_id=13131

Jones, J. (1959). *Pastor Jones Meets Rev. M. J. Divine: Better Known As Father Divine*. Indianapolis, IN: Brothers Printing Company. Alternative Considerations. https://jonestown.sdsu.edu/wp-content/uploads/2013/10/01-04-JJFatherDivine.pdf

(n.d.). "The Letter Killeth." Alternative Considerations. https://jonestown.sdsu.edu/?page_id=14111

(1972?). "Redwood Valley Sermon." Video. Collection of Laurie Efrein.

(1977). "An Untitled Collection of Reminiscences by Jim Jones." Alternative Considerations. https://jonestown.sdsu.edu/?page_id=13143

Jones, L. (n.d.). "The Writings of Lynetta Jones." Alternative Considerations. https://jonestown.sdsu.edu/?page_id=62772

Jones, M. (n.d.a). "Undated Recollection by Marceline Jones." Alternative Considerations. https://jonestown.sdsu.edu/?page_id=18692

(n.d.b). "The Words of Marceline Jones." Alternative Considerations. https://jonestown.sdsu.edu/?page_id=13155

Jones, M., & L. Jones. (1975). "A Joint Statement of Marceline Jones and Lynetta Jones." May 20. Alternative Considerations. https://jonestown.sdsu.edu/?page_id=18690

"Jonestown Governmental Responsibility." (n.d.). Alternative Considerations. https://jonestown.sdsu.edu/wp-content/uploads/2013/10/3c-JTGovtResp.pdf

"Jonestown Petition to Block Rep. Ryan." (1978). Alternative Considerations. https://jonestown.sdsu.edu/?page_id=13929

The Living Word. (1972). 1, no. 1. Alternative Considerations. https://jonestown.sdsu.edu/?page_id=14090

"Peoples Temple Ad." (1955). *Indianapolis Recorder*. December 10. Alternative Considerations. www.flickr.com/photos/peoplestemple/40424746703/in/album-72157706000175671

(1956a). *Indianapolis Recorder*. May 19. Alternative Considerations. www.flickr.com/photos/peoplestemple/47337437222/in/album-72157706000175671

(1956b). *Indianapolis Recorder*. June 2. Alternative Considerations. www.flickr.com/photos/peoplestemple/47337437072/in/album-72157706000175671

(1956c). *Indianapolis News*, June 9. Alternative Considerations. www.flickr.com/photos/peoplestemple/47390272231/in/album-72157706000175671

"Peoples Temple Meetings with the Soviet Embassy in Georgetown, Guyana, 1978." (1978). Alternative Considerations. https://jonestown.sdsu.edu/?page_id=112381

"The Peoples Temple Songbook." (n.d.). Alternative Considerations. https://jonestown.sdsu.edu/?page_id=18793

"Petition to Move to the Soviet Union." (1978). Alternative Considerations. https://jonestown.sdsu.edu/?page_id=13121

Press Release. (1976). "Social Ministry for Social Justice." Alternative Considerations. https://jonestown.sdsu.edu/wp-content/uploads/2013/10/02-news09-26-76.pdf

Prokes, M. (1979). "Michael Prokes' Suicide Note." Alternative Considerations. https://jonestown.sdsu.edu/wp-content/uploads/2013/10/MichaelProkes SuicideNote.pdf

"Proposed By-Laws for Wings of Deliverance, Inc." (n.d.). Alternative Considerations. https://jonestown.sdsu.edu/wp-content/uploads/2013/10/01-WODBylaws.pdf

"Resolution of Peoples Temple to Block Rep. Ryan from Entering Jonestown." (1978). Alternative Considerations. https://jonestown.sdsu.edu/?page_id=13932

"Resolution to Establish Agricultural Mission." (1973). Alternative Considerations. https://jonestown.sdsu.edu/?page_id=13068

Roller, E. (1975). "Edith Roller Journals." August. Alternative Considerations. https://jonestown.sdsu.edu/?page_id=35673

(1976a). "Edith Roller Journals." February 1–15. Alternative Considerations. https://jonestown.sdsu.edu/?page_id=35675

(1976b). "Edith Roller Journals." May. Alternative Considerations. https://jonestown.sdsu.edu/?page_id=35678

(1976c). "Edith Roller Journals." October. Alternative Considerations. https://jonestown.sdsu.edu/?page_id=35683

(1976d). "Edith Roller Journals." December. Alternative Considerations. https://jonestown.sdsu.edu/?page_id=35685

(2013). "Edith Roller Journals." Alternative Considerations. https://jonestown.sdsu.edu/?page_id=35667

"September Ag Reports." (1978). Alternative Considerations. https://jonestown.sdsu.edu/wp-content/uploads/2013/10/6SeptFarmRallyRpts.pdf

"Statement of 13 November 1978." (1978). Alternative Considerations. https://jonestown.sdsu.edu/?page_id=13934

Stoen, T. O. (1972). "Tim Stoen Affidavit of February 6, 1972." Alternative Considerations. https://jonestown.sdsu.edu/?page_id=13836

"US Addresses for People Emigrating to Guyana." (1977). Alternative Considerations. https://jonestown.sdsu.edu/wp-content/uploads/2013/10/PTaddressesinUS.pdf

Secondary Sources

Albanese, C. L. (2007). *A Republic of Mind and Spirit: A Cultural History of American Metaphysical Religion*. New Haven, CT: Yale University Press.

Appel, W. (1983). *Cults in America: Programmed for Paradise*. New York: Henry Holt.

Baird, L. (2004). "Notes on Jonestown Carpet, 2004." *the jonestown report* 6 (October). https://jonestown.sdsu.edu/?page_id=32669

Barkun, M. (2013). *A Culture of Conspiracy: Apocalyptic Visions in Contemporary America*. 2nd ed. Berkeley: University of California Press.

Beck, D. (2005a). "The Healings of Jim Jones." *the jonestown report* 7 (November). https://jonestown.sdsu.edu/?page_id=32369

(2005b). "A Peoples Temple Life." *the jonestown report* 7 (November). https://jonestown.sdsu.edu/?page_id=32367

(2011). "Talking with Cults: Conversations with a Video Director." *the jonestown report* 13 (October). https://jonestown.sdsu.edu/?page_id=29273

(2012). "Expenditures by Peoples Temple in Guyana." *the jonestown report* 14 (October). https://jonestown.sdsu.edu/?page_id=34223

(2013). "Administration." Jonestown Research. Alternative Considerations. https://jonestown.sdsu.edu/?page_id=35901

Black, E. (2012). "Farming Utopia: The Promised Lands of the Peace Mission and Peoples Temple." *the jonestown report* 14 (October). https://jonestown.sdsu.edu/?page_id=34228

(2014). "Utopian Justice, Righteousness, and Divine Socialism: The Politics of Father Jehovia, Father Divine, and Jim Jones and of the Cause They Headed." *jtr bulletin* 16 (November). https://jonestown.sdsu.edu/?page_id=61363

(2015). "Atheistic Gods and Divine Leaders of the Religion of Social Justice: The Theology of Father Jehovia, Father Divine and Jim Jones." *the jonestown report* 17 (November). https://jonestown.sdsu.edu/?page_id=65056

Blakey, P. (2018). "Snapshots from a Jonestown Life." *the jonestown report* 20 (October). https://jonestown.sdsu.edu/?page_id=81310

"The Books of the Jonestown Library." (2012). *the jonestown report* 14 (October). https://jonestown.sdsu.edu/?page_id=34227

Brandou, A. (2007). "Artist Depicts Jonestown Lessons in Childrens Animals." *the jonestown report* 9 (November). https://jonestown.sdsu.edu/?page_id=33148

Breslauer, G. (2021). "Cults of Our Hegemony: An Inventory of Left-Wing Cults." *the jonestown report* 23 (October). https://jonestown.sdsu.edu/?page_id=111267

Bromley, D. G. (2002). "Dramatic Denouements." In D. G. Bromley & J. G. Melton, eds., *Cults, Religion, and Violence*. Cambridge: Cambridge University Press, pp. 11–41.

Carew, J. (2014). "Jonestown Revisited." Alternative Considerations. https://jonestown.sdsu.edu/?page_id=61391

Carter, T. (2008). "Thirty Years Later." *the jonestown report* 10 (October). https://jonestown.sdsu.edu/?page_id=31349

Cartmell, M. (2010). "A Mother-in-Law's Blues." *the jonestown report* 12 (October). https://jonestown.sdsu.edu/?page_id=30232

Chidester, D. (1988). "Rituals of Exclusion and the Jonestown Dead." *Journal of the American Academy of Religion* 56(4), 681–702.

   (2003). *Salvation and Suicide: An Interpretation of Jim Jones, the Peoples Temple, and Jonestown*. Bloomington: Indiana University Press.

Chireau, Y. P. (2003). *Black Magic: Religion and African American Conjuring Traditions*. Berkeley: University of California Press.

Clifton, L. (2012). "1. at jonestown." In K. Young & M. S. Glaser, eds., *The Collected Poems of Lucille Clifton 1965–2010*. Rochester, NY: BOA Editions, pp. 267–9.

Collins, J. (2018). "Jim Jones and the Postwar Healing Revival." *the jonestown report* 20 (October). https://jonestown.sdsu.edu/?page_id=81621

Crist, R. E. (1981). "Jungle Geopolitics in Guyana: How a Communist Utopia That Ended in Massacre Came to Be Sited." *American Journal of Economics and Sociology* 40, 107–14.

"Cult Song Includes Temple Images." (2011). *the jonestown report* 13 (October). https://jonestown.sdsu.edu/?page_id=29275

Cusack, C. (2020). "Anne Hamilton-Byrne and the Family: Charisma, Criminality and Media in the Construction of an Australian 'Cult' Leader." *Nova Religio* 24(1), 31–54.

Cyprès, D. (2021). "Concept Album Considers Jonestown Tragedy through Tape Archive." Alternative Considerations. https://jonestown.sdsu.edu/?page_id=112525

D'Aguiar, F. (1998). *Bill of Rights*. London: Chatto and Windus.

Enroth, R. (1979). *The Lure of the Cults*. Chappaqua, NY: Christian Herald Books.

Farrell, M. T. (2012). "Peoples Temple As Plot Device." *the jonestown report* 14 (October). https://jonestown.sdsu.edu/?page_id=34251

    (2018). "Escaping the Event Horizon (A Rebuttal to John Judge's *The Black Hole of Guyana*)." *the jonestown report* 20 (October). https://jonestown .sdsu.edu/?page_id=80865

Feltmate, D. (2016). "Perspective: Rethinking New Religious Movements beyond a Social Problems Paradigm." *Nova Religio* 20(2), 82–96.

    (2018). "Peoples Temple: A Lost Legacy for the Current Moment." *Nova Religio* 22(2), 115–36.

Folk, Holly. (2018). "Divine Materiality: Peoples Temple and Messianic Theologies of Incarnation and Reincarnation." *Nova Religio* 22(2), 15–39.

Gillespie, C. (2011). *Jonestown: A Vexation*. Detroit, MI: Lotus Press.

Gordon, T. (2012). "Peoples Temple Agricultural Project on Canvas." *the jonestown report* 14 (October). https://jonestown.sdsu.edu/?page_id= 34360

Griffith, R. M. (2001). "Body Salvation: New Thought, Father Divine, and the Feast of Material Pleasures." *Religion and American Culture* 11(2), 119–53.

Guinn, Jeff. (2017). *The Road to Jonestown: Jim Jones and Peoples Temple*. New York: Simon and Schuster.

Hall, J. R. (1988). "Collective Welfare As Resource Mobilization in Peoples Temple: A Case Study of a Poor People's Religious Social Movement." *Sociological Analysis* 49 Supplement, 64S–77S.

    (1995). "Public Narratives and the Apocalyptic Sect: From Jonestown to Mt. Carmel." In S. A. Wright, ed., *Armageddon in Waco: Critical Perspectives on the Branch Davidian Conflict*. Chicago: University of Chicago, pp. 205–35.

    (2004). *Gone from the Promised Land: Jonestown in American Cultural History*. New Brunswick, NJ: Transaction Books.

Hall, J. R., with P. D. Schuyler & S. Trinh. (2000). *Apocalypse Observed: Religious Movements and Violence in North America, Europe and Japan*. London: Routledge.

Harpe, D. (2010). "My Experience with Jim Jones and Peoples Temple." *the jonestown report* 12 (October). https://jonestown.sdsu.edu/?page_ id=30265

Harrell, D. E., Jr. (1975). *All Things Are Possible: The Healing and Charismatic Revivals in Modern America*. Bloomington: Indiana University Press.

Harris, D., & A. J. Waterman. (2004). "To Die for the Peoples Temple: Religion and Revolution after Black Power." In R. Moore, A. B. Pinn & M. R. Sawyer, eds.,

Peoples Temple and Black Religion in America. Bloomington: Indiana University Press, pp. 103–22.

Harris, W. (1996). *Jonestown*. London: Faber and Faber.

Harrison, M. F. (2004). "Jim Jones and Black Worship Traditions." In R. Moore, A. B. Pinn & M. R. Sawyer, *Peoples Temple and Black Religion in America.* Bloomington: Indiana University Press, pp. 123–38.

Hassan, S. (2019). *The Cult of Trump.* New York: Free Press.

Hatcher, C. (1989). "After Jonestown: Survivors of Peoples Temple." In R. Moore & F. M. McGehee III, eds., *The Need for a Second Look at Jonestown.* Lewiston, NY: Edwin Mellen Press, pp. 127–46.

Hollis, T. M. (2004). "Peoples Temple and Housing Politics in San Francisco." In R. Moore, A. B. Pinn & M. R. Sawyer, eds., *Peoples Temple and Black Religion in America.* Bloomington: Indiana University Press, pp. 81–102.

Hougan, J. (2003). "The Secret Life of Jim Jones: A Parapolitical Fugue." *Alternative Considerations.* https://jonestown.sdsu.edu/?page_id=16572

Hutchinson, S. (2015). *White Nights, Black Paradise.* Los Angeles: Infidel Books.

Isaacson, B. (2015). "'Mao Tse Tung Said', by Alabama 3: Jim Jones, Irony, and Revolutionary Politics." *the jonestown report* 17 (November). https://jonestown.sdsu.edu/?page_id=64818

James, C. (2020). Interview with Preston Jones. *Military Response to Jonestown.* www.youtube.com/watch?v=BCPAeyIhgFo

Johnson, M. R. (2019). Interview with Preston Jones. *Military Response to Jonestown.* www.youtube.com/watch?v=K9zKk3RhFGc

Johnson, P. D. (1979). "Dilemmas of Charismatic Leadership: The Case of the People's Temple." *Sociological Analysis* 40(4), 315–23.

Jones, S. (2005). "Marceline/Mom." *the jonestown report* 7 (November). https://jonestown.sdsu.edu/?page_id=32388

Judge, J. (1985). "The Black Hole of Guyana: The Untold Story of the Jonestown Massacre." Alternative Considerations. https://jonestown.sdsu.edu/?page_id=78282

Kenyatta, M. I. (2004) [1979]. "America Was Not Hard to Find." In R. Moore, A. B. Pinn & M. R. Sawyer, eds., *Peoples Temple and Black Religion in America.* Bloomington: Indiana University Press, pp. 158–65.

Kerns, P., with D. Wead. (1979). *People's Temple, People's Tomb.* Plainfield, NJ: Logos International.

Kilduff, M., & R. Javers. (1978). *Suicide Cult: The Inside Story of the Peoples Temple Sect and the Massacre in Guyana.* New York: Bantam.

Kilduff, M., & P. Tracy. (1977). "Inside Peoples Temple." *New West Magazine* (August), 30–8. Also at Alternative Considerations. https://jonestown.sdsu.edu/?page_id=14025

King, J. (2018). "Jonestown's Victims Have a Lesson to Teach Us, So I Listened." *Mother Jones* 16 (November). https://www.motherjones.com/politics/2018/11/jonestowns-victims-have-a-lesson-to-teach-us-so-i-listened-peoples-temple-anniversary-40/

Klippenstein, K. D. (2009). "Peoples Temple As Christian History: A Corrective Interpretation." *the jonestown report* 11 (November). https://jonestown.sdsu.edu/?page_id=30827

(2015). "Jones on Jesus: Who Is the Messiah." *International Cultic Studies Journal* 6, 34–47. https://jonestown.sdsu.edu/?page_id=99153

(2018). "Spiritual Siblings: The Functions of New Religions in Peoples Temple Doctrine." *Nova Religio* 22(2), 40–64.

Knoll, J. L., IV. (2008). "The Jonestown Tragedy As Familicide-Suicide." *the jonestown report* 10 (October). https://jonestown.sdsu.edu/?page_id=31403

Kohl, L. J. (2005). "*The People's Temple*: A Review." *the jonestown report* 7 (November). https://jonestown.sdsu.edu/?page_id=32332

(2010). *Jonestown Survivor: An Insider's Look*. Bloomington, IN: iUniverse.

Kohl, L. J., ed. (2017). "Guyana after Jonestown: A Special Section." *the jonestown report* 19 (November). https://jonestown.sdsu.edu/?page_id=70268

Krause, C. A. (1978). *Guyana Massacre: The Eyewitness Account*. New York: Berkley.

Krebs, M. V. (1978). Memo to Ashley Hewitt, December 3. In *The Assassination of Representative Leo J. Ryan and the Jonestown, Guyana Tragedy*. Committee on Foreign Affairs, US House of Representatives, May 15, 1979. Washington, DC: US Government Printing Office, pp. 133–6.

Krinsky, C., ed. (2016). *The Ashgate Research Companion to Moral Panics*. New York: Routledge.

Kwayana, E., ed. (2016). *A New Look at Jonestown: Dimensions from a Guyanese Perspective*. Los Angeles: Carib House.

Lane, M. (1980). *The Strongest Poison*. New York: Hawthorn Books.

Lasaga, J. I. (1980). "Death in Jonestown: Techniques of Political Control by a Paranoid Leader." *Suicide and Life-Threatening Behavior* 10(4), 210–13.

Layton, C. (1978). "Carolyn Layton's Analysis of Future Prospects." Alternative Considerations. https://jonestown.sdsu.edu/?page_id=13115

Layton, D. (1998). *Seductive Poison: A Jonestown Survivor's Story of Life and Death in the Peoples Temple*. New York: Anchor Books.

Levi, K. (1982a). "Jonestown and Religious Commitment in the 1970s." In K. Levi, ed., *Violence and Religious Commitment: Implications of Jim Jones's People's Temple Movement*. University Park: Pennsylvania State University Press, pp. 3–20.

Levi, K., ed. (1982b). *Violence and Religious Commitment: Implications of Jim Jones's People's Temple Movement*. University Park: Pennsylvania State University Press.

Lewis, G. T. (1979). *Gather with the Saints at the River: The Jonestown Holocaust of 1978: A Descriptive and Interpretive Essay on Its Ultimate Meaning from a Caribbean Viewpoint*. Rio Piedras: University of Puerto Rico Institute of Caribbean Studies.

Lewis, J. R. (2005). "The Solar Temple 'Transits': Beyond the Millennialist Hypothesis." In J. R. Lewis & J. A. Peterson, eds., *Controversial New Religions*. New York: Oxford University Press, pp. 295–317.

Lincoln, C. E., & L. H. Mamiya. (2003). *The Black Church in the African American Experience*. Durham, NC: Duke University Press.

(2004). "Daddy Jones and Father Divine: The Cult As Political Religion." In R. Moore, A. B. Pinn & M. R. Sawyer, eds., *Peoples Temple and Black Religion in America*. Bloomington: Indiana University Press, pp. 28–46.

Lorde, A. (2000). *The Collected Poems of Audre Lorde*. New York: W. W. Norton.

Maaga, M. M. (1998). *Hearing the Voices of Jonestown*. Syracuse, NY: Syracuse University Press.

Mabee, C. (2008). *Promised Land: Father Divine's Interracial Communities in Ulster County, New York*. Fleischmanns, NY: Purple Mountain Press.

Maguire, J., & M. L. Dunn. (1978). *Hold Hands and Die: The Incredibly True Story of the People's Temple and the Reverend Jim Jones*. New York: Dale Books.

Matthews, L. K., & G. K. Danns. (1980). "Communities and Development in Guyana: A Neglected Dimension in Nation Building." Georgetown, Guyana: University of Guyana. Reprinted in 2016 as "The Jonestown Plantation." In Eusi Kwayana, ed., *A New Look at Jonestown: Dimensions from a Guyanese Perspective*. Los Angeles: Carib House, pp. 82–95.

Matthews, W. (1978). Memo to [Ashley] Hewitt, December 4. In *The Assassination of Representative Leo J. Ryan and the Jonestown, Guyana Tragedy*. Committee on Foreign Affairs, US House of Representatives, May 15, 1979. Washington, DC: US Government Printing Office, pp. 139–42.

McGehee, F. M., III. (2002). "Was There Social Security Fraud in Jonestown: A Special Report." *the jonestown report* 4 (November). https://jonestown.sdsu.edu/?page_id=32943

(2013a). "What Are White Nights? How Many of Them Were There?" Alternative Considerations. https://jonestown.sdsu.edu/?page_id=35371

(2013b). "Peoples Temple and Gordon Lindsay." Alternative Considerations. https://jonestown.sdsu.edu/?page_id=13147

(2013c). "Was Peoples Temple Responsible for the Deaths of Some of Its Former Members?" Alternative Considerations. https://jonestown.sdsu.edu/?page_id=35343

(2018). "Teri Buford O'Shea: Surviving Betrayal. *Alternative Considerations* https://jonestown.sdsu.edu/?page_id=84682

(2019). "Did Peoples Temple Commit Welfare Fraud Especially with the Foster Children under Its Care?" Alternative Considerations. https://jonestown.sdsu.edu/?page_id=35358

(2021a). "Who Is Philip Blakey? Was He a Mercenary for the CIA in Angola?" Alternative Considerations. https://jonestown.sdsu.edu/?page_id=112002

(2021b). "'Drinking the Kool-Aid' As a Tool for Education: An Editorial." *the jonestown report* 23 (October). https://jonestown.sdsu.edu/?page_id=111356

Melton, J. G. (2003). "Pentecostal Family." In J. Gordon Melton, ed., *Encyclopedia of American Religions*. 7th ed. Detroit, MI: Gale Division of Cengage Learning, pp. 83–90.

Melton, J. G., & D. G. Bromley. (2009). "Violence and New Religions: An Assessment of Problems, Progress, and Prospects in Understanding the NRM–Violence Connection." In M. al-Rasheed & M. Shterin, eds., *Dying for Faith: Religiously Motivated Violence in the Contemporary World*. London: I. B. Tauris, pp. 27–41.

Mills, J. (1979). *Six Years with God: Life inside Reverend Jim Jones's Peoples Temple*. New York: A & W.

Moore, R. (1985). *A Sympathetic History of Jonestown*. Lewiston, NY: Edwin Mellen Press.

(1986). *The Jonestown Letters: Correspondence of the Moore Family, 1970–1985*. Lewiston, NY: Edwin Mellen Press.

(2002). "Reconstructing Reality: Conspiracy Theories about Jonestown." *Journal of Popular Culture* 36(2), 200–20.

(2011). "Narratives of Persecution, Suffering, and Martyrdom: Violence in Peoples Temple and Jonestown." In J. R. Lewis, ed., *Violence and New Religious Movements*. New York: Oxford University Press, pp. 95–111.

(2013). "Rhetoric, Revolution, and Resistance in Jonestown, Guyana." *Journal of Religion and Violence* 1(3), 303–21.

(2017). "An Update on the Demographics of Jonestown." *the jonestown report* 19 (November). https://jonestown.sdsu.edu/?page_id=70495

(2018a). *Understanding Jonestown and Peoples Temple.* Westport, CT: Praeger.

(2018b). "The Erasure and Reinscription of African Americans from the Jonestown Narrative." *Communal Societies* 38(2), 161–84.

(2018c). "Godwin's Law and Jones' Corollary: The Problem of Using Extremes to Make Predictions." *Nova Religio* 22(3), 145–54.

(2018d). *Beyond Brainwashing: Perspectives on Cult Violence.* Cambridge: Cambridge University Press.

(2018e). "Jonestown at 40: The Real Conspiracy Is More Disturbing Than the Theories." *Religion Dispatches.* https://rewirenewsgroup.com/religion-dis patches/2018/11/16/jonestown-at-40-the-real-conspiracy-is-more-disturb ing-than-the-theories. Also available at Alternative Considerations, https:// jonestown.sdsu.edu/?page_id=84726.

(2018f). "The Forensic Investigation of Jonestown Conducted by Dr. Leslie Mootoo: A Critical Analysis." *the jonestown report* 20 (October). https:// jonestown.sdsu.edu/?page_id=80811

(2021). "Apocalyptic Groups and Charisma of the Cadre." In J. P. Zúqete, ed., *The Routledge International Handbook of Charisma.* New York: Routledge, pp. 277–87.

(2022a). "From Resistance to Terror: The Open Secret of Jonestown." In H. B. Urban & P. C. Johnson, eds., *The Routledge Handbook of Religion and Secrecy.* New York: Routledge, pp. 175–86.

(2022b). "Peoples Temple and Jonestown Enclaves." World Religions and Spirituality Project. https://wrldrels.org/2022/01/18/peoples-temple-and-jonestown-enclaves

Moore, R., A. B. Pinn, & M. R. Sawyer, eds. (2004). *Peoples Temple and Black Religion in America.* Bloomington: Indiana University Press.

Morris, A. (2018). "Preliminary Notes on a Possible Antecedent: Andrew Jackson Davis." *the jonestown report* 20 (October). https://jonestown .sdsu.edu/?page_id=81671

Mrett, T. (2020). "The Communism of Jonestown: Marxist or Utopian?" *the jonestown report* 22 (October). https://jonestown.sdsu.edu/?page_id=102313

Naipaul, S. (1980). *Journey to Nowhere: A New World Tragedy.* New York: Simon and Schuster.

Nelson, S. (2006). *Jonestown: the Life and Death of Peoples Temple.* New York: Firelight Media.

Nesci, D. A. (1999). *The Lessons of Jonestown: An Ethnopsychoanalytical Study of Suicidal Communities*. Rome: Universo Publishing.

(2018). *Revisiting Jonestown: An Interdisciplinary Study of Cults*. Lanham, MD: Lexington Books.

Newton, H. P. (1973). *Revolutionary Suicide*. New York: Writers and Readers.

Nugent, J. P. (1979). *White Night*. New York: Rawson, Wade.

Parker, P. (1985). *JONESTOWN and Other Madness*. Ithaca, NY: Firebrand Books.

Pinn, A. B. (2004). "Peoples Temple As Black Religion: Re-imagining the Contours of Black Religious Studies." In R. Moore, A. B. Pinn & M. R. Sawyer, eds., *Peoples Temple and Black Religion in America* Bloomington: Indiana University Press, pp.1–27.

Pinn, A. B., ed. (2001). *By These Hands: A Documentary History of African American Humanism*. New York: New York University Press.

Poster, A. (2019). "Jonestown: An International Story of Diplomacy, Détente, and Neglect, 1973–1978." *Diplomatic History* 43(2), 305–31.

Reichert, J., & J. T. Richardson. (2012). "Decline of a Moral Panic: A Social Psychological and Socio-legal Examination of the Current Status of Satanism." *Nova Religio* 16(2), 47–63.

Reiterman, T., with J. Jacobs. (1982). *Raven: The Untold Story of the Rev. Jim Jones and His People*. New York: E. P. Dutton.

Reston, J., Jr. (1981). *Our Father Who Art in Hell*. New York: Times Books.

Robbins, T. (1989). "The Second Wave of Jonestown Literature: A Review Essay." In R. Moore & F. M. McGehee, III, eds., *New Religious Movements, Mass Movements, and Peoples Temple: Scholarly Perspectives on a Tragedy*. Lewiston, NY: Edwin Mellen Press, pp. 113–34.

Robbins, T., & D. Anthony. (1995). "Sects and Violence: Factors in Enhancing the Volatility of Marginal Religious Movements." In S. A. Wright, ed., *Armageddon in Waco: Critical Perspectives on the Branch Davidian Conflict*. Chicago, IL: University of Chicago, pp. 236–59.

Rodney, W. (1979). "Jonestown: A Caribbean/Guyanese Perspective." Alternative Considerations. https://jonestown.sdsu.edu/?page_id=67276

Rose, S. (1979). *Jesus and Jim Jones*. New York: Pilgrim Press.

Scheeres, J. (2011). *A Thousand Lives: The Untold Story of Hope, Deception, and Survival at Jonestown*. New York: Free Press.

scott, d. a. (2010). "Reading the Language of Jonestown." *the jonestown report* 12 (October). https://jonestown.sdsu.edu/?page_id=30237

(2022). *Marrow*. Lexington: University Press of Kentucky.

Shearer, H. (2018). "'Verbal Orders Don't Go: Write It!': Building and Maintaining the Promised Land." *Nova Religio* 22(2), 65–92.

(2020). "Marceline Jones." *Women in the World's Religions and Spirituality Project.* https://wrldrels.org/2020/09/08/marceline-jones

Shojael, M. (2016). "An Image That Thinks." *the jonestown report* 18 (November). https://jonestown.sdsu.edu/?page_id=67822

(2017). "A Vague Murmur of Art." *the jonestown report* 19 (November). https://jonestown.sdsu.edu/?page_id=71187

Singer, M. T. (2003). *Cults in Our Midst.* Rev. ed. San Francisco: Jossey-Bass.

Smith, A., Jr. (1982). *The Relational Self: Ethics and Therapy from a Black Church Perspective.* Nashville, TN: Abingdon Press.

(2004). "An Interpretation of Peoples Temple and Jonestown: Implications for the Black Church." In R. Moore, A. B. Pinn & M. R. Sawyer, eds., *Peoples Temple and Black Religion in America.* Bloomington: Indiana University Press, pp. 47–54.

Smith, E. (2021). *Back to the World: A Life after Jonestown.* Fort Worth: Texas Christian University.

Stroup, K. (2007). "Could It Happen Again?" *the jonestown report* 9 (November). https://jonestown.sdsu.edu/?page_id=33228

Taylor, M. (2015). "'One Hand Can't Clap': Guyana and North Korea, 1974– 1985." *Journal of Cold War Studies* 17(1) 41–63.

Thielmann, B., with D. Merrill. (1979). *The Broken God.* Elgin, IL: David C. Cook.

Thornbrough, E. L. (2000). *Indiana Blacks in the Twentieth Century.* Edited and with a final chapter by L. Ruegamer. Bloomington: Indiana University Press.

Thrash, H. (Catherine). (1995). *The Onliest One Alive: Surviving Jonestown, Guyana.* As told to Marian K. Towne. Indianapolis, IN: Marian K. Towne.

Tretyakov, S. (2015). "Music of Q932 Speaks to Real Cult in American Life." *the jonestown report* 17 (November). https://jonestown.sdsu.edu/?page_id=64799

Ulman, R. B., & W. Abse. (1983). "The Group Psychology of Mass Madness: Jonestown." *Political Psychology* 4(4), 637–61.

Wagner-Wilson, L. (2008). *Slavery of Faith.* Bloomington, IN: iUniverse.

Weaver, C. D. (1987). *The Healer-Prophet, William Marrion Branham: A Study of the Prophetic in American Pentecostalism.* Macon, GA: Mercer University Press.

Weightman, J. M. (1984). *Making Sense of the Jonestown Suicides: A Sociological History of Peoples Temple.* Lewiston, NY: Edwin Mellen Press.

Wessinger, C. (2000). *How the Millennium Comes Violently: From Jonestown to Heaven's Gate.* New York: Seven Bridges Press.

(2008). "The Problem Is Totalism, Not 'Cults': Reflections on the Thirtieth Anniversary of the Deaths in Jonestown." *the jonestown report* 10 (October). https://jonestown.sdsu.edu/?page_id=31459

Wessinger, C., ed. (2011). *The Oxford Handbook of Millennialism*. New York: Oxford University Press.

Whittle, T. (2018a). "Unanswered Questions about Jonestown." June 10. Scientologists Taking Action against Discrimination. www.standleague.org/newsroom/news/unanswered-questions-about-jonestown.html

(2018b). "Unanswered Questions about Jonestown: Part Two." July 16. Scientologists Taking Action against Discrimination. www.standleague.org/newsroom/blog/unanswered-questions-about-jonestown-part-two.html

Wooden, K. (1981). *The Children of Jonestown*. New York: McGraw-Hill.

Woollett, L. E. (2018). *Beautiful Revolutionary*. Brunswick, VIC: Scribe.

Acknowledgments

A number of people helped bring this book to fruition whom I would like to acknowledge. I deeply appreciate the wisdom of John R. Hall, Jeff Guinn, Margo Kitts, and Catherine Wessinger, to whom I am greatly indebted. John Collins provided assistance in understanding the influence of William Branham on Jim Jones. Brenna Norman at the San Juan Public Library tracked down books I needed through interlibrary loan, and Anna Culbertson, head of Special Collections in the library at San Diego State University, expedited acquisition of photographs. I thank the staff at Cambridge University Press and those devoted to producing the Elements series in New Religious Movements: Beatrice Rehl, James Baker, Priyadharshini Samidurai, N. P. Vibhu Prathima, and the anonymous copyeditors and compositors who worked on this volume. I would also like to acknowledge my coeditor in the Cambridge Elements series on New Religious Movements, James R. Lewis. Jim has developed a remarkable series that I feel privileged to work on. Most important, my husband, Fielding McGehee III, is a veritable encyclopedia of information about Peoples Temple and Jonestown. I could not have written this book without daily consultations with him. Finally, I dedicate this book to the memory of Laura Johnston Kohl, Vernon Gosney, and Don Beck. Their insights into Peoples Temple and Jonestown are sorely missed.

Cambridge Elements

New Religious Movements

Series Editors

James R. Lewis
Wuhan University

James R. Lewis is Professor of Philosophy at Wuhan University, China. He currently edits or co-edits four book series, is the general editor for the *Alternative Spirituality and Religion Review* and the associate editor for the *Journal of Religion and Violence*. His publications include *The Cambridge Companion to Religion and Terrorism* (Cambridge University Press 2017) and *Falun Gong: Spiritual Warfare and Martyrdom* (Cambridge University Press 2018).

Rebecca Moore
San Diego State University

Rebecca Moore is Emerita Professor of Religious Studies at San Diego State University. She has written numerous books and articles on Peoples Temple and the Jonestown tragedy. Publications include *Beyond Brainwashing: Perspectives on Cultic Violence* (Cambridge University Press 2018) and *Peoples Temple and Jonestown in the Twenty-First Century* (Cambridge University Press 2022). She is reviews editor for *Nova Religio*, the quarterly journal on new and emergent religions published by University of California Press.

About the Series

Elements in New Religious Movements go beyond cult stereotypes and popular prejudices to present new religions and their adherents in a scholarly and engaging manner. Case studies of individual groups, such as Transcendental Meditation and Scientology, provide in-depth consideration of some of the most well known, and controversial, groups. Thematic examinations of women, children, science, technology, and other topics focus on specific issues unique to these groups. Historical analyses locate new religions in specific religious, social, politicial, and cultural contexts. These examinations demonstrate why some groups exist in tension with the wider society and why others live peaceably in the mainstream. The series highlights the differences, as well as the similarities, within this great variety of religious expressions. To discuss contributing to this series please contact Professor Moore.

Cambridge Elements ≡

New Religious Movements

Elements in the Series